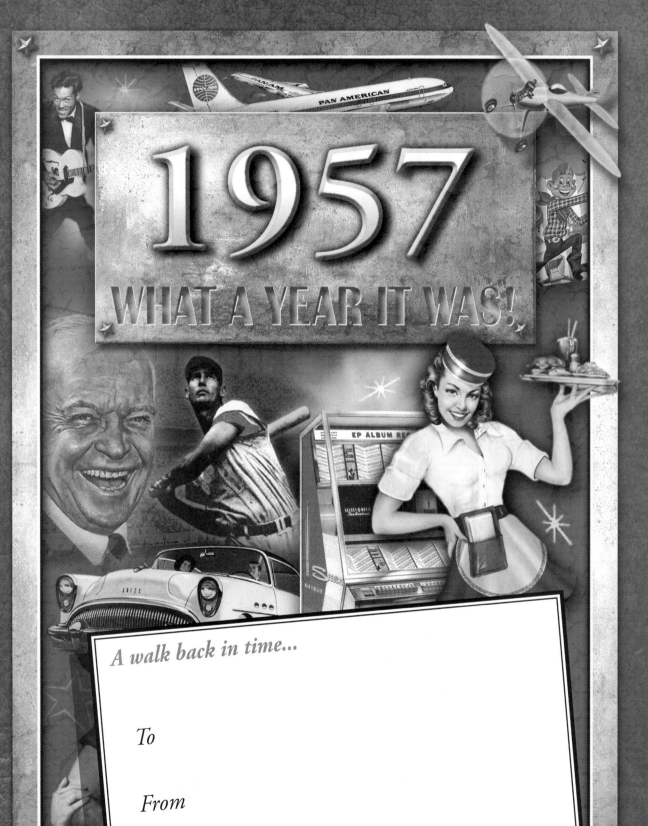

1957
WHAT A YEAR IT WAS!

PAN AMERICAN

EP ALBUM RE

A walk back in time...

To

From

FLICKBACK

Dedicated to America's Korean War veterans,
with gratitude for their sacrifices.

Publisher • Art Worthington
Designer • Peter Hess
Writing & Research • Peter Hess
Facilitator • Pamela Thomas

www.FLICKBACK.com
(800) 541-3533

Contents

Arts & Entertainment

NIGHTS OF CABIRIA PG

LE NOTTI DI CABIRIA

Giulietta Masina
BEST ACTRESS
CANNES FILM FESTIVAL

Newly restored in a sparkling NEW 35MM PRINT

The British Film Institute in association with Canal+ Distribution present a Dino de Laurentiis-Les Films Marceau Production.
GIULIETTA MASINA in FEDERICO FELLINI'S NIGHTS OF CABIRIA
Screenplay by FEDERICO FELLINI ENNIO FLAIANO and TULLIO PINELLI Additional Dialogue by PIER PAOLO PASOLINI Music by NINO ROTA
Produced by DINO DE LAURENTIIS Directed by FEDERICO FELLINI

A number of foreign directors have big years with award-winning films. Italian **Federico Fellini's** *Nights of Cabiria*, concerning a charming prostitute, is an international hit. Swedish director **Ingmar Bergman's** serious cinematic inquiries into the nature of life and death, *The Seventh Seal* and *Wild Strawberries*, receive worldwide critical acclaim. **Satyajit Ray**, from India, completes *Aparajito*, the second in his trilogy about the appealing boy, Apu. *Throne of Blood* is Japanese director **Akira Kurosawa's** re-staging of *Macbeth* as a Samurai epic.

A INGMAR BERGMAN FILM
THE SEVENTH SEAL

DRIVE-IN NIGHTS

For many Americans, the movie-going experience means parking under the stars in drive-in theaters, which number around 4,000 nationwide. In the privacy and relative anonymity of their cars, audiences indulge their taste for "shocking" juvenile delinquent and girls-gone-bad double features. Teasing advertisements featuring shapely women and black leather jacket-clad rumblers often promise more thrills than the low-budget potboilers can deliver. Among the titles packing them in: *The Delinquents, The Girl in Black Stockings, Hot Rod Rumble* ("The slick chicks who fire up the big wheels!"), *Motorcycle Gang, Naked Paradise, Reform School Girl, Rock All Night* (Some have to dance... some have to kill!) and *Young and Dangerous*. Even comic **Jerry Lewis** gets a piece of the action as a shaky bad boy in *The Delicate Delinquent*.

THE AMAZING TRUE STORY OF DELINQUENT GIRLS!

REFORM SCHOOL GIRL

GLORIA CASTILLO · ROSS FORD · EDWARD BYRNES
Story and Screenplay by EDWARD BERNDS · Executive Producer JAMES H. NICHOLSON · Produced by ROBERT J. GURNEY Jr. & SAMUEL Z. ARKOFF
Directed by EDWARD BERNDS · A CARMEL PRODUCTION · AN AMERICAN INTERNATIONAL PICTURE

DER OVER HAWAII

ROCK ALL NIGHT

THE PLATTERS
THE BLOCKBUSTERS
A SUNSET PRODUCTION starring
ER · RUSSELL JOHNSON · ABBY DALTON
by ROGER CORMAN · Executive Producer JAMES H. NICHOLSON · Screenplay by
CHARLES GRIFFIN · AN AMERICAN INTERNATIONAL PICTURE

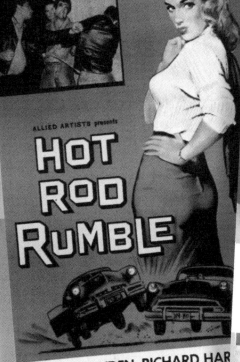

ALLIED ARTISTS presents

HOT ROD RUMBLE

LEIGH SNOWDEN · RICHARD HAR
WRIGHT KING with JOEY FORMAN · BRETT HALSEY
Produced by NORMAN T. HERMAN · Directed by LESLIE H. MARTINSON · Written

SHE WAS EVERY INCH A TEASING, TAUNTING, "COME-ON" BLONDE...

THE GIRL IN BLACK STOCKINGS

AND SHE MADE EVERY INCH PA OF

LEX BARKER · ANNE BANCROFT · MAMIE VA
RON RANDELL · MARIE WINDSOR · JOHN DEHNER with JOHN
Screenplay by RICHARD LANDAU · sic by Les Baxter · Executive Producer AUBREY SCHENCK · Direct
A BEL-AIR PRODUCTION · Released by United Artists

BLOOD OF DRACULA
HOT ROD RUMBLE

at the MOVIES

MARILYN MONROE starring with LAURENCE OLIVIER in Warner Bros.

The Prince and the Showgirl

Some countries have a medal for Everything.

LIFE IS IN THEIR HANDS— DEATH IS ON THEIR MINDS

IT EXPLODES LIKE 12 STICKS OF DYNAMITE!

HENRY FONDA

12 ANGRY MEN

with LEE J. COBB · ED BEGLEY and E. G. MARSHALL · JACK WARDEN · Story and Screenplay by REGINALD ROSE
Directed by SIDNEY LUMET · Produced by HENRY FONDA and REGINALD ROSE · Associate Producer GEORGE JUSTIN
An ORION-NOVA Production · Released thru UNITED ARTISTS

"A MAGNIFICENT, MOVING FILM!"
LIFE Magazine

"DESTINED TO BECOME A CLASSIC!"
LOOK Magazine

HECHT-HILL and LANCASTER
present

BURT LANCASTER
TONY CURTIS

"Sweet Smell of Success"

The Motion Picture That Will Never Be Forgiven— Or Forgotten!

MARLON BRAN

COLUMBIA PICTURES
presents
A SAM SPIEGEL PRODUCTION

WILLIAM HOLDEN
ALEC GUINNESS · JACK HAWK

in

"THE BRIDGE ON THE RIVER KWAI"

CINEMASCOPE   TECHNICOLOR®

with SESSUE HAYAKAWA · JAMES DONALD · ANN SEARS and introducing GEOFFREY HORNE
Directed by DAVID LEAN · Screenplay by PIERRE BOULLE Based on his Novel

TECHNI
TECHNIC
REGIA
JOSHUA

SAYONAR

20th CENTURY-FOX presents

CARY GRANT
DEBORAH KERR

in
Leo McCarey's **AN AFFAIR TO REMEMBER**

COLOR BY DE LUXE
CINEMASCOPE

RICHARD DENNING · NEVA PATTERSON · CATHLEEN NESBITT · ROBERT Q. LEWIS · CHARLES WATTS · FORTUNATO BONANOVA
PRODUCED by JERRY WALD · LEO McCAREY · DELMER DAVES and LEO McCAREY

AUDREY **HEPBURN**

FRED **ASTAI**

FUNNY FACE

in

KAY THOMPSON

with MICHEL AUCLAIR · ROBERT FLEMYNG
MUSIC and LYRICS by GEORGE and IRA GERSHWIN

An Affair To Remember
The Bridge On The River Kwai
Desk Set
Edge Of The City
Enemy Below
A Face In The Crowd
Funny Face
Gunfight At The O.K. Corral
A Hatful Of Rain
Heaven Knows, Mr. Allison
Island In The Sun
The James Dean Story
A King In New York
Les Girls
Love In The Afternoon
Man Of A Thousand Faces
Man On Fire
Old Yeller
The Pajama Game
Pal Joey
Paths Of Glory
Peyton Place
The Prince And The Showgirl
Raintree County
Saint Joan
Sayonara
Silk Stockings
The Spirit Of St. Louis
The Sun Also Rises
The Sweet Smell Of Success
Tammy And The Bachelor
This Could Be The Night
Three Faces Of Eve
Twelve Angry Men
Witness For The Prosecution

1957

An abundant year for

HORROR & SCI-FI

TOP STARS
of '57

Rock **Hudson**
John **Wayne**
Sophia **Loren**
Marilyn **Monroe**
Frank **Sinatra**
Gary **Cooper**
William **Holden**
James **Stewart**
Jerry **Lewis**
Yul **Brynner**

NEW STARS
of '57

Carroll **Baker**
Pat **Boone**
Anita **Ekberg**
Martha **Hyer**
John **Kerr**
Jayne **Mansfield**
Don **Murray**
Paul **Newman**
Anthony **Perkins**
Elvis **Presley**

John Wayne

Marilyn Monroe

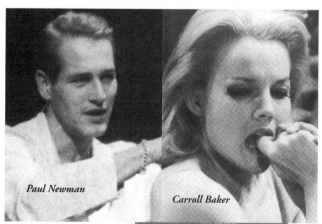

Paul Newman

Carroll Baker

Elvis Presley's second film, *Loving You*, is released, quickly followed by *Jailhouse Rock*, which spawns the #1 hit record of the same name.

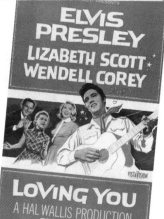

10

The Academy Awards

"And The Winner Is..."

Oscars Presented in 1957

BEST PICTURE
AROUND THE WORLD IN 80 DAYS

BEST ACTOR
YUL BRYNNER, *The King And I*

BEST ACTRESS
INGRID BERGMAN, *Anastasia*

BEST DIRECTOR
GEORGE STEVENS, *Giant*

BEST SUPPORTING ACTOR
ANTHONY QUINN, *Lust for Life*

BEST SUPPORTING ACTRESS
DOROTHY MALONE, *Written On The Wind*

BEST SONG
"WHATEVER WILL BE, WILL BE (QUE SERA, SERA)," *The Man Who Knew Too Much*

Yul Brynner

1957 Favorites *(Oscars Presented in 1958)*

BEST PICTURE
THE BRIDGE ON THE RIVER KWAI

BEST ACTOR
ALEC GUINNESS, *The Bridge On The River Kwai*

BEST ACTRESS
JOANNE WOODWARD, *The Three Faces Of Eve*

BEST DIRECTOR
DAVID LEAN, *The Bridge On The River Kwai*

BEST SUPPORTING ACTOR
RED BUTTONS, *Sayonara*

BEST SUPPORTING ACTRESS
MIYOSHI UMEKI, *Sayonara*

BEST SONG
"ALL THE WAY," *The Joker Is Wild*

Miyoshi Umeki

Fans gather outside the Pantages Theatre in Hollywood to watch their favorite movie stars arrive for the

29th Annual Academy Awards.

A special ovation greets **Janet Gaynor**, who was the first to receive the Best Actress award in 1928.

Beaming **Robert Stack** is nominated as Best Supporting Actor for his performance in *Written On The Wind*.

Anthony Quinn receives his second Oscar nomination for his performance in *Lust For Life*.

Jack Lemmon presents the Best Supporting Actress award to Dorothy Malone for her role in *Written On The Wind*.

An overjoyed Miss Malone makes her acceptance speech.

In Ingrid Bergman's absence, Cary Grant accepts the Best Actress award for her performance in *Anastasia*.

Yul Brynner receives his Oscar from Anna Magnani for the Best Actor for his performance in *The King And I*.

Mitzi Gaynor presents the Best Picture award to director Mike Todd for his production, *Around The World In 80 Days*.

Dorothy Malone and Anthony Quinn show off their awards.

Memorable Lines

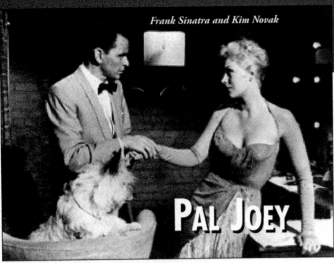

Frank Sinatra and Kim Novak

PAL JOEY

Linda English: *Why do people drink when you feel so awful the morning after?*

Joey Evans: *Maybe because it feels so good the night before.*

Linda English: *What did I do last night?*
Joey Evans: *You kissed me.*
Linda English: *I wasn't myself.*
Joey Evans: *Whoever you were, you were great!*

PATHS OF GLORY

Kirk Douglas

General Broulard: *Colonel Dax! You will apologize at once or I shall have you placed under arrest!*

Colonel Dax: *I apologize... for not being entirely honest with you. I apologize for not revealing my true feelings. I apologize, sir, for not telling you sooner that you're a degenerate, sadistic old man. And you can go to hell before I apologize to you now or ever again!*

WITNESS FOR THE PROSECUTION

Charles Laughton and Marlene Dietrich

Leonard Vole: *But this is England, where I thought you never arrest, let alone convict, people for crimes they have not committed.*

Sir Wilfrid: *We try not to make a habit of it.*

Sir Wilfrid: *I am constantly surprised that women's hats do not provoke more murders.*

Sweet Smell of Success

Tony Curtis and Burt Lancaster

Sam: *But Sidney, you make a living. Where do you want to get?*

Sidney Falco: *Way up high, Sam, where it's always balmy. Where no one snaps his fingers and says, "Hey, Shrimp, rack the balls!" or, "Hey, mouse, mouse, go out and buy me a pack of butts." I don't want tips from the kitty. I'm in the big game with the big players... In brief, from now on, the best of everything is good enough for me.*

J.J. Hunsecker: *You're dead, son. Get yourself buried.*

Celebrities Attend The Premiere In New York Of "The Great Man" Starring Jose Ferrer

Opera star ROBERT MERRILL and his wife attend the premiere.

A smiling SAMMY DAVIS, JR. attends festivities alone.

AL MORGAN, author of the best selling novel on which the movie is based, attends the premiere with VICKY DUGAN.

Pals ROBERT ALDA (right), STUBBY KAYE (center) and BILLY GOLDBERG attend this festive event.

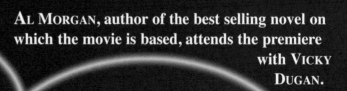

BATTLE HYMN Premieres In Korean War Hero Colonel Dean Hess' Hometown With Two Days Of Festivities

Marietta, Ohio stages the greatest civic celebration in its history to welcome **Colonel Dean Hess** and the premiere of his dramatic film biography, *Battle Hymn*.

A lavish banquet is given honoring the Colonel.

Festivities continue for two days including this parade honoring all those associated with the film.

Rock Hudson, who plays the Colonel in the film, makes his way through a most enthusiastic crowd.

Rock Hudson, pictured with **Dan Duryea**.

The parson who became an ace airman saved thousands of Korean orphans from capture by the reds.

Celebrating Founder's Day, Marietta College bestows an honorary degree on Rock Hudson.

The festivities culminate with the premiere and the biggest crowd ever gathering outside the theatre.

Rock Hudson, Colonel Hess and a City Father smile at the crowd as they get ready to enter the theatre.

Now you can run your color-slide show from anywhere in the room!

NEW ARGUS REMOTE CONTROL SLIDE PROJECTOR

Complete with carrying case, slide magazine and 15 ft. of control cord.

ONLY $ **85.00** Most dealers offer budget terms . . . as little as $8.50 down.

Just relax in your favorite easy chair or sofa . . . anywhere in the room . . . while you run a really professional color-slide show with this great new Argus Remote Control Projector.

You just press the button on the compact, hand-fitting control switch to *automatically* show, change and return your slides to their proper places in the magazine. And you can change from remote to direct control any time you wish.

This finest of all Argus projectors also offers you all these other precision features: an exclusive new light condenser system—to give you brighter, clearer pictures; a new wide-angle lens—to give you big, life-size pictures even in a small room.

In addition, there's a compact, 36-slide aluminum magazine—to protect slides from dirt and dog-earing; a powerful blower—to keep slides and projector cool during long showings; a handy Slide Editor—to let you preview slides and arrange them in story-telling sequence.

Stop in at your Argus dealer's soon. Let him show you how beautiful color slides can be . . . and how easily and inexpensively you can show them . . . with this new Argus Remote Control Projector.

Color slides cost surprisingly little . . . only 5 cents more than ordinary black-and-white prints—just about a third as much as color prints! You see your slides big as life on a screen, and when you're not showing them, they're stored in compact aluminum magazines.

Argus projector prices start at $39.50. All Argus projectors, including the $39.50 Argus 300 (shown at right), have an exclusive optical system that gives you bigger pictures even in a small room. The Argus Automatic Projector—without remote control is priced at only $62.50.

argus ®

Argus Cameras, Ann Arbor, Michigan.
Division of Sylvania Electric Products Inc.

WORLD'S NO. 1 NAME IN COLOR-SLIDE PHOTOGRAPHY

BORN IN 1957 ★
LEVAR BURTON ★
STEVE BUSCEMI ★
ETHAN COEN ★
STEPHEN FRY ★
MELANIE GRIFFITH ★ SPIKE LEE
DANIEL-DAY LEWIS ★ FRANCES
McDORMAND ★ KELLY McGILLIS
KEVIN POLLAK ★ THERESA RUSSELL
★ ROBERT TOWNSEND
★ JOHN TURTURRO
★ MARIO VAN PEEBLES
★ RACHEL WARD

Frances McDormand

Daniel-Day Lewis

☆ **Rita Hayworth** fulfills her 20-year contract with Columbia Pictures, returning to the screen after a three-year absence.

☆ *Island In The Sun* starring **James Mason**, **Dorothy Dandridge**, **Joan Fontaine** and **Harry Belafonte** is the first film to depict an interracial romance.

☆ Well-scrubbed singer **Pat Boone** makes his screen debut with **Shirley Jones** in *April Love*.

☆ 50% of the nation's teenagers see at least one movie a week.

☆ 1,200 movie theaters close as audiences turn to other sources of entertainment, including television.

☆ Hanna-Barbera Productions is created when "Tom & Jerry" animators **Joseph Barbera** and **William Hanna** join forces.

HOLLYWOOD BIDS A FOND FAREWELL

Iconic actor **Humphrey Bogart** dies at 57, leaving an unmatched body of film work including HIGH SIERRA, THE MALTESE FALCON, CASABLANCA, THE CAINE MUTINY and his Academy Award-winning performance in THE AFRICAN QUEEN.

Oliver Hardy, half of the greatest comedy team in the history of movies, dies at age 65.

Oliver Hardy, right, with Stan Laurel

Louis B. Mayer, co-founder of MGM and architect of Hollywood's star system, dies at 72.

Director/actor **Erich von Stroheim** is dead at age 71.

Silent screen star **Norma Talmadge** dies at 60.

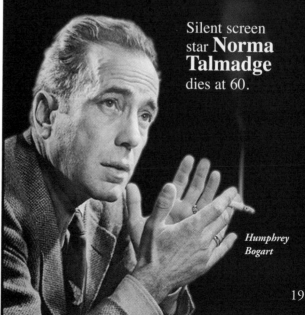
Humphrey Bogart

So simple to tune—even a child can do it. The *Aldrich* (above) in limed oak grained finish (21CS781). $495.

Big as life. Even the lowest priced RCA Victor Big Color set gives a huge 254 square inches of viewable picture—crisp and clear in black-and-white or Color.

All the colors of life. RCA Victor Big Color TV gives Color so natural, so alive—you have to see it to believe it. It's a completely new experience in home entertainment.

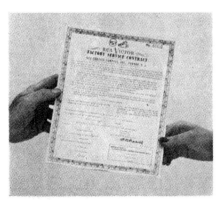

Practical and dependable. Big Color TV service is low-cost—RCA Victor Factory Service Contracts available in most areas, but only to owners of RCA Victor TV.

"LIVING COLOR" AT $495 IS NOW BEST TV BUY–IT'S LIKE 2 SETS IN 1

See Color every night — see black-and-white shows, too. RCA Victor Big Color is today's best TV investment!

Here is double-value Color TV at the lowest price in RCA Victor history. Now you and your family will see every program *exactly* as it is broadcast. . . . big Color shows in breath-taking "Living Color"—all regular programs in crisp, clear black-and-white.
New "Color-Quick" tuning—simple, fast, accurate. Turn two knobs and the screen blossoms out in Color. Even a child can tune it.

Your choice of 10 Big Color models—from table model to full-door console in contemporary or traditional styling.
See "Living Color" with your own eyes at your RCA Victor dealer's soon. Ask him about easy budget terms on any Big Color set—your present TV may even cover the down payment!

Manufacturer's nationally advertised VHF list price shown. UHF optional, extra. Prices and specifications subject to change. **At your service:** RCA Victor Factory Service Contracts from $39.95 (90 days).

RCA VICTOR
RADIO CORPORATION OF AMERICA
RCA PIONEERED AND DEVELOPED COMPATIBLE COLOR TV

Like 2 sets in 1 because it's RCA Victor *Compatible* Color. Color shows in Color—all others in black-and-white. This is today's common-sense investment in TV.

20

Television

MUSICAL CHAIRS

Busy **Steve Allen**, the original host of *The Tonight Show* since its 1954 debut, departs the program in January to concentrate on other projects, including his own Sunday night show opposite **Ed Sullivan**. **Ernie Kovacs**, who handles *Tonight's* hosting duties Monday and Tuesday nights, leaves as

Steve Allen

well. NBC decides to try a version of *Tonight* modeled on its popular morning *Today Show*. The new chatty news format *Tonight! America After Dark*, hosted by **Jack Lescoulie**, quickly proves unsuccessful and is

replaced mid-year by *Tonight starring Jack Paar*, with the new popular host reverting to the original talk show format.

Meanwhile, after spending almost all of his 4 1/2 years with **Dave Garroway** on the *Today Show*, mascot **J. Fred Muggs**, the world's most successful chimpanzee, quits to seek greener trees. Having amassed a fortune between salary and product endorsements, the wealthy Mr. Muggs is the envy of a lot of show biz folks.

- *Maverick* and *Have Gun Will Travel* are among 10 new Westerns making their TV debuts.

- *The Price Is Right*, hosted by **Bill Cullen**, graduates from daytime to prime time television.

- **Howard Cossell** gets his first regular daily sports wrap-up program.

- **Kermit the Frog** makes his debut on the *Tonight Show*.

Leave it to Beaver debuts on CBS, beginning a 7-year run.

TV's Cleaver family: mom Barbara Billingsly, dad Hugh Beaumont, big brother Tony Dow and Jerry Mathers as the Beaver.

Lucille Ball

Dick Clark takes Philadelphia favorite *American Bandstand* national on ABC.

The *I Love Lucy* gang begins taping one-hour shows called *The Lucy-Desi Comedy Hour*. Meanwhile, Lucille Ball's *Desilu Productions* reaches basic agreement to purchase RKO Studios.

Elvis Presley makes final appearance on *The Ed Sullivan Show*.

DJ **Alan Freed** hosts first prime-time rock special, the *Rock 'n' Roll Show*.

Alan Freed

BORN IN 1957 ★
DAN CASTELLANETA ★ KATIE COURIC ★ FRAN DRESCHER ★ LEEZA GIBBONS ★

Homer Simpson (voiced by Dan Castellaneta)

STEVE HARVEY ★ MATT LAUER ★ BERNIE MAC ★ PAUL REISER ★ RAY ROMANO ★ VANNA WHITE

Katie Couric

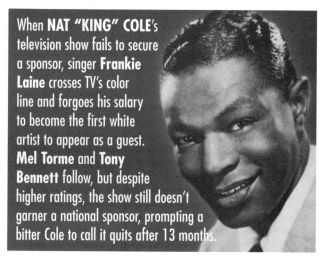

When **NAT "KING" COLE**'s television show fails to secure a sponsor, singer **Frankie Laine** crosses TV's color line and forgoes his salary to become the first white artist to appear as a guest. **Mel Torme** and **Tony Bennett** follow, but despite higher ratings, the show still doesn't garner a national sponsor, prompting a bitter Cole to call it quits after 13 months.

PRIMETIME LINEUP

		7:00	7:30	8:00	8:30	9:00	9:30	10:00	10:30
SATURDAY	ABC	Local	Keep It in the Family	Country Music Jubilee		Lawrence Welk's Dancing Party		Mike Wallace Interviews	
	CBS	Local	Perry Mason		Dick & the Duchess	Gale Storm Show	Have Gun, Will Travel	Gunsmoke	
	NBC	Local	People Are Funny	Perry Como Show		Polly Bergen Show	Giselle MacKenzie Show	What's It For	Your Hit Parade
SUNDAY	ABC	You Asked for It	Maverick		Bowling Stars	Open Hearing	All-American Football Game of the Week		
	CBS	Lassie	Jack Benny/ Bachelor Father	Ed Sullivan Show		G.E. Theater	Alfred Hitchcock Presents	$64,000 Challenge	What's My Line
	NBC	Original Amateur Hour	Sally	Steve Allen Show		Dinah Shore Chevy Show		Loretta Young Show	
MONDAY	ABC	Local	American Bandstand	Guy Mitchell Show	Bold Journey	Voice of Firestone	Lawrence Welk's Top Tunes		
	CBS	Local	Adventures of Robin Hood	Burns and Allen	Arthur Godfrey's Talent Scouts	Danny Thomas Show	December Bride	Studio One in Hollywood	
	NBC	Local	The Price is Right	Restless Gun	Tales of Wells Fargo	Twenty-One	Turn of Fate	Suspicion	
TUESDAY	ABC	Local	Cheyenne/Sugarfoot		Wyatt Earp	Broken Arrow	Telephone Time	West Point Story	
	CBS	Local	Name That Tune	Phil Silvers Show	Eve Arden Show	To Tell the Truth	Red Skelton Show	$64,000 Question	Assignment Foreign Legion
	NBC	Local	Nat "King" Cole Show	Eddie Fisher Show/ George Gobel Show		Meet McGraw	Bob Cummings Show	The Californians	
WEDNESDAY	ABC	Local	Disneyland		Tombstone Territory	Ozzie and Harriet	Walter Winchell File	Wednesday Night Fights	
	CBS	Local	I Love Lucy	Big Record		The Millionaire	I've Got a Secret	Armstrong Circle Theatre/ U.S. Steel Hour	
	NBC	Local	Wagon Train			Kraft Television Theatre		This is Your Life	
THURSDAY	ABC	Local	Circus Boy	Zorro	Real McCoys	Pat Boone	O.S.S.	Navy Log	
	CBS	Local	Sgt. Preston of the Yukon	Harbormaster	Climax		Playhouse 90		
	NBC	Local	Tic Tac Dough	You Bet Your Life	Dragnet	People's Choice	Tennessee Ernie Ford	Lux Show w/ Rosemary Clooney	Jane Wyman Show
FRIDAY	ABC	Local	Adventures of Rin Tin Tin	Adventures of Jim Bowie	Patrice Munsel Show	Frank Sinatra Show	Date with the Angels	Colt .45	
	CBS	Local	Leave it to Beaver	Trackdown	Dick Powell's Zane Grey Theatre	Mr. Adams & Eve	Schlitz Playhouse	The Lineup	Person to Person
	NBC	Local	Saber of London	Court of Last Resort	Life of Riley	M Squad	Thin Man	Gillette Cavalcade of Sports	

SYLVANIA'S revolutionary 110° TV tube whittles the bulk from BIG SCREEN portables

The Slimmest Case

New wide-angle tube cuts 7″ from former depth. Case is even slimmer than small-screen sets.

The Biggest Screen

New 17″ (overall diagonal) tube gives you a larger picture than other 17″ tubes. You get a full 150 square inches of viewable picture.

The Clearest Picture

Sylvania's new "S-110" chassis builds added power for extra reach in fringe areas; high voltage assures sharper focus.

SYLVANIA 17″ SLIM JIM PORTABLE

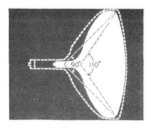

Here is why Slim Jim is slimmer: Because Sylvania has pioneered the development of this new 110° wide-angle picture tube, Sylvania alone can offer you the newest, slimmest, most compact of all 17″ portable TV sets.

Here's another TV "first" by Sylvania: the biggest picture in portable TV—in a case so slender it rests anywhere! This family-size set adjusts to its surroundings as easily as tiny-screen sets.

Until now, big-screen portables were deep and bulky because ordinary picture tubes are so deep. But Sylvania engineers have developed a powerful, wide-angle tube that whittles away awkward bulk.

Thanks to Sylvania's exclusive 110° Deflection Picture Tube, Slim Jim is slimmer, lower, lighter—a pleasure to look at.

You can own a Sylvania 17″ Slim Jim portable for as little as **$139.95***

*Manufacturer's suggested retail price

New excitement in "personal" radios
Sylvania's "THUNDERBIRD" 7-Transistor Portable Radio

New, exciting, trim as a sports car, completely tubeless. Sylvania-engineered to pull in distant stations with a clarity new in "personal" radios. Its 7 tiny transistors last far longer than tubes. Room-filling tone—or optional earphones. *Hear it—you'll be amazed!*

SPECIAL INTRODUCTORY OFFER— with new Sylvania 17″ SLIM JIM portables

The exclusive swivel base transforms your Sylvania portable into a console with living-room manners. It swivels the set completely around— a full 360°—angles the picture to your own point of view, makes your favorite chair the best seat in the house.

For a limited time, this handsomely made swivel base is yours for only **$4.88***

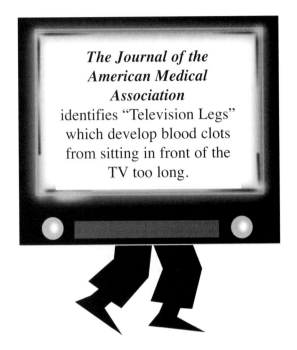

The Journal of the American Medical Association identifies "Television Legs" which develop blood clots from sitting in front of the TV too long.

The FCC accepts applications for pay-TV.

California studios produce 60% of network programming, attracting some of the most talented New York playwrights and actors.

Charles Van Doren, champion on the *Twenty-One* quiz show, wins $129,000, lands on the cover of *Time* magazine and receives 500 marriage proposals. Van Doren denies cheating, saying "It's silly and distressing to think that people don't have more faith in quiz shows." It is later revealed in testimony before a Senate subcommittee that he was supplied with answers in advance.

Truth Or Consequences is the first videotaped program.

The **Eisenhower/Nixon** inauguration is the first videotaped national broadcast carried by NBC.

A report published in Denmark indicates there are more than 50 million TV receivers in use throughout the world with the United States being the number one user at 38 million and Canada number two at two million. Norway and Bulgaria finish last with 500 receivers each.

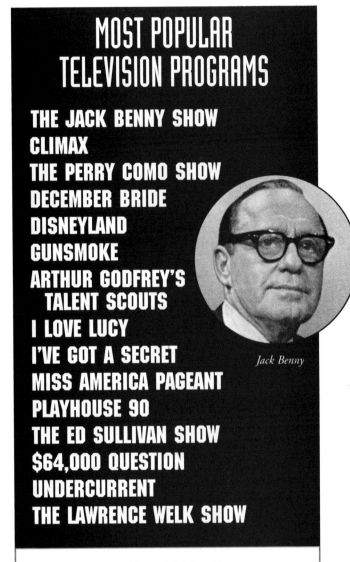

MOST POPULAR TELEVISION PROGRAMS

THE JACK BENNY SHOW
CLIMAX
THE PERRY COMO SHOW
DECEMBER BRIDE
DISNEYLAND
GUNSMOKE
ARTHUR GODFREY'S TALENT SCOUTS
I LOVE LUCY
I'VE GOT A SECRET
MISS AMERICA PAGEANT
PLAYHOUSE 90
THE ED SULLIVAN SHOW
$64,000 QUESTION
UNDERCURRENT
THE LAWRENCE WELK SHOW

Jack Benny

EMMY AWARDS

Best Series: (one hour)	CAESAR'S HOUR
Best Series: (half-hour)	THE PHIL SILVERS SHOW
Best Actor In A Series:	ROBERT YOUNG — FATHER KNOWS BEST
Best Actress In A Series:	LORETTA YOUNG — THE LORETTA YOUNG SHOW
Best Comedian:	SID CEASAR — CAESAR'S HOUR
Best Comedienne:	NANETTE FABRAY — CAESAR'S HOUR

"LOOK OUT, GRACIE!

WITH ZENITH SPACE COMMAND TV I CAN CHANGE PROGRAMS FROM ACROSS THE ROOM"...

George!..You wouldn't dare!'

THE DEAUVILLE, Model AX013

ONLY ZENITH HAS SPACE COMMAND, THE REMOTE CONTROL UNIT THAT TUNES TV BY "SILENT SOUND"...

JUST TOUCH A BUTTON TO ...

• shut off the sound of long, annoying commercials while the picture remains on the screen
• turn TV on and off
• change channels 'either direction.

No Wires, No Batteries, No Transistors ...

NOTHING BETWEEN YOU AND THE SET BUT SPACE!

Now tune TV from your lounge chair... anywhere in the room! At the touch of a button, the control unit in your hand emits a "Silent Sound" which only the electronic ear of your Space Command receiver can hear. Instantly your set responds! Automatically, each channel comes in sharper than ever before on Zenith's revolutionary new "Sunshine" Picture Tube.

The tone, too, is brilliantly superior, because Zenith's four High Fidelity Speakers, mounted on the sides of your picture screen, fill the room with true "living" sound.

Select the perfect Space Command TV set for your room from Zenith's new Decorator Group in Traditional, Modern, and Provincial style cabinets. You'll have the finest in television plus the joy of Space Command Remote TV Control. Not an extra cost accessory, it's built right into your set!

BURNS AND ALLEN SHOW
Seen every week over CBS Television Network

ZENITH RADIO CORPORATION
Chicago 39, Illinois

The quality goes in before the Zenith name goes on.
Backed by 38 years of leadership in radionics exclusively.
Also makers of Radio, High Fidelity Instruments and Fine Hearing Aids.

QUALITY BY

Zenith
SPACE COMMAND TV

The Royalty of Television

28

Popular Music

HITMAKERS

'57 HITMAKERS

Elvis Presley
Dominating the charts with multiple #1 hits

3 hits reach #1

Pat Boone

Sam Cooke

3 successive #1 R&B hits

"You Send Me"

Fats Domino

"Wake Up Little Susie," "Bye Bye Love"

"Tammy"

Everly Brothers

Debbie Reynolds

Jerry Lee Lewis

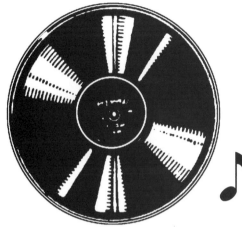

Harry Belafonte

1957 POPULAR SONGS

A Fine Romance	Ella Fitzgerald & Louis Armstrong
All Shook Up	Elvis Presley
April Love	Pat Boone
A White Sport Coat (And A Pink Carnation)	Marty Robbins
Banana Boat Song (Day O)	Harry Belafonte
Blueberry Hill	Fats Domino
Butterfly	Andy Williams
Bye Bye Love	The Everly Brothers
Chances Are	Johnny Mathis
Diana	Paul Anka
Friendly Persuasion	Pat Boone
Honeycomb	Jimmy Rodgers
Jailhouse Rock	Elvis Presley
Little Darlin'	The Diamonds
Love Letters In The Sand	Pat Boone
Magic Moments	Perry Como
Maria	from "West Side Story"
Marianne	Harry Belafonte
Party Doll	Buddy Knox
Peggy Sue	Buddy Holly
Raunchy	Bill Justis
Rock & Roll Music	Chuck Berry
Round And Round	Perry Como
Seventy-Six Trombones	from "The Music Man"
So Rare	Jimmy Dorsey Orch.
That'll Be The Day	The Crickets
The Story Of My Life	Marty Robbins
Tammy	Debbie Reynolds
Tonight	from "West Side Story"
Too Much	Elvis Presley
Wake Up Little Susie	The Everly Brothers
Whole Lot Of Shakin' Going On	Jerry Lee Lewis
You Send Me	Sam Cooke

31

Ella Fitzgerald

Peggy Lee

Gene Autry

Frank Sinatra

Popular Singers

(A SAMPLING)

PERRY COMO
BING CROSBY
EDDIE FISHER
PEGGY LEE
DEAN MARTIN
GISELE MACKENZIE
PATTY PAGE
FRANK SINATRA
ELLA FITZGERALD

Recently departed from Columbia Records after being forced to record substandard material, FRANK SINATRA sends a telegram to the House Judiciary Sub-committee investigating music industry corruption, accusing Columbia's A&R head MITCH MILLER of soliciting large sums of money from writers whose songs he recorded.

NEW TALENT

Paul Anka
Patsy Cline
Sam Cooke
The Crickets
Bobby Darin
The Everly Brothers
Connie Francis
Buddy Holly
Brenda Lee
Jerry Lee Lewis
Johnny Mathis
Ricky Nelson
Conway Twitty
Jackie Wilson

Top Concert Stars

(A SAMPLING)

GENE AUTRY
PAT BOONE
SMILEY BURNETTE
BOB HOPE
RICKY NELSON
ELVIS PRESLEY
JOHNNIE RAY
ROY ROGERS
JIMMY WAKELY

- ♪ **Pat Boone** performs at President Eisenhower's inaugural ball and signs a $1 million television deal.

- ♪ **Little Richard** shakes up the music world when he announces he is giving up Rock 'n' Roll for religion.

- ♪ 15-year old Canadian **Paul Anka** writes "Diana," a song dedicated to his childhood babysitter.

- ♪ The **Everly Brothers'** "Wake Up Little Susie" is banned in Boston because it is thought the song alludes to a sexual affair.

- ♪ **Buddy Holly and the Crickets** are the first white act to play Harlem's Apollo Theatre in New York.

- ♪ A first for Rock 'n' Roll— **Sonny James** and **Tab Hunter** both reach No. 1 with "Young Love."

- ♪ An **Alan Freed** show starring **The Platters**, **The Teenagers** and **Buddy Knox** breaks all attendance records at New York's Paramount Theatre.

- ♪ 4,000 Rock 'n' Roll fans break through police barriers to greet **Bill Haley** at London's Waterloo Station.

- ♪ British fans vote **Pat Boone** The World's Outstanding Singer; **Elvis Presley**, World's Outstanding Musical Personality; **Doris Day**, World's Top Female Singer; and **The Platters**, World's Top Group.

Bill Haley and his Comets

Little Richard

Buddy Holly and the Crickets

Teenagers all over the world love Elvis and show their enthusiasm by buying over sixteen million copies of his eight records and sending him over forty thousand letters a week.

JOHN LENNON and PAUL McCARTNEY Meet For The First Time At A Church Garden Party.

Jazz

Downbeat's

Top Performers

Benny Goodman

BENNY GOODMAN
COUNT BASIE
LES BROWN
MODERN JAZZ QUARTET
BARNEY KESSEL
RAY BROWN
ERROL GARNER
JIMMY GUIFFRE
MILES DAVIS
HERBIE MANN
ELLA FITZGERALD
FRANK SINATRA
HI-LO'S

Miles Davis

Sonny Rollins releases a pair of albums, *Way Out West* and *A Night at the Village Vanguard*, featuring the pioneering modern saxophonist accompanied solely by bass and drums. The *Vanguard* album marks the first live recording issued from the legendary New York nightspot.

Idiosyncratic pianist **Thelonious Monk** finally recovers the cabaret card maliciously confiscated by the NYPD in 1951, enabling him to resume club performances. He wastes no time, launching a 6-month residency at the Five Spot with his new quartet which features **John Coltrane** on sax.

Miles Davis has disbanded his quintet and embarked on what will prove to be a fruitful partnership spanning several albums with arranger **Gil Evans**. Their first joint endeavor, the adventurous *Miles Ahead*, showcases the trumpeter's work in front of a big band.

New releases from Miles Davis, Charles Mingus, Modern Jazz Quartet, Thelonious Monk and Sonny Rollins

Billie Holiday *appears on the CBS TV program* The Sound of Jazz, *singing* Fine and Mellow *with support from (l-r)* ***Lester Young****,* ***Ben Webster*** *and* ***Gerry Mulligan****.*

LOUIS ARMSTRONG *angrily cancels his U.S. government-sponsored tour of the Soviet Union in protest over America's treatment of southern blacks.*

JIMMY DORSEY, jazz clarinetist and famed bandleader who scored 23 hits in the early 1940's dies of cancer at 53 just as his recording of *So Rare* reaches # 2 on the Hit Parade.

TOP SELLING COUNTRY RECORDS

Young Love
SONNY JAMES

There You Go
JOHNNY CASH

Gone
FERLIN HUSKY

A White Sport Coat (and a Pink Carnation)
MARTY ROBBINS

Honky Tonk Song
WEBB PIERCE

Four Walls
JIM REEVES

My Shoes Keep Walking Back to You
RAY PRICE

PLEASE MR. TALLY MAN, TALLY ME ROY-AL-TIES

With **Harry Belafonte**'s album *Calypso* one of the biggest selling records in RCA Victor history, do-it-yourself Calypso kits consisting of bongo drums, gourd and maracas sell briskly at $24.50 each.

DON'T QUIT YOUR DAY JOB

Tab Hunter	*Young Love*
Robert Mitchum ..	*Mama Look-a-Boo-Boo*
Jerry Lewis	*Rock-a-Bye Your Baby With a Dixie Melody*
Anthony Perkins ..	*A Little Love Can Go a Long, Long Way*
Grace Kelly	*True Love*
Fess Parker	*Davy Crockett*

♪ San Francisco poets Lawrence Ferlinghetti and Kenneth Patchen are among poets fusing their poetry with Jazz.

♪ Berry Gordy, Jr. starts Motown Records.

♪ West Indian music becomes the rage in the United States.

♪ Hal David and Burt Bacharach collaborate on their first two big hits—"Magic Moments" and "The Story Of My Life."

BORN IN 1957 ★

LAURA BRANIGAN ★ NICK CAVE ★ SHEILA E. ★ GLORIA ESTEFAN ★ VINCE GILL ★ MARLON JACKSON ★ PATTY LOVELESS ★ LYLE LOVETT ★ DONNY OSMOND ★ SID VICIOUS

Sheila E.

35

When better automobiles are built Buick will build them

Solid click on the TROJAN campus

We previewed the B-58 Buick at the University of Southern California — and drew a more enthusiastic turnout than a movie crew on location.

What sent the students the most was that new Miracle Ride, plus Air-Poise Suspension.*

They couldn't get over the way this Buick levels itself, no matter how heavy the load, or where you place it.

They marveled at the way the worst bumps and potholes seemed to disappear beneath the wheels.

And what brought the widest grins of glee was the way this big B-58 sailed up the winding canyon roads without a trace of slew or sway.

When we tallied up the comments, "It's the greatest!" was the mildest.

So — go see what the hubbub's all about, at your Buick dealer's now.

BUICK *Division of* GENERAL MOTORS

Air-Poise Suspension optional at extra cost on all Series.

TRY THE MIRACLE RIDE OF—

THE AIR BORN B-58 BUICK

See TALES OF WELLS FARGO, Monday Nights, NBC-TV and THE PATRICE MUNSEL SHOW, Friday Nights, ABC-TV

36

Classical Music

Europe's New Divas

●

Anita Cerquetti *(Italy)*
Clara Petrella *(Italy)*
Irene Dalis *(U.S.)*
Eugenia Ratti *(Italy)*

PASSINGS

Sibelius

Finnish composer JEAN SIBELIUS, who dropped out of law school to pursue music, is dead at 91.

ARTURO TOSCANINI, brilliant Italian conductor who headed La Scala and the Metropolitan Opera, conducting the world premieres of *Pagliacci, La Boheme* and *Girl Of The Golden West*, dies at 89.

BENIAMO GIGLI, one of the most popular operatic tenors of the century, dies at 71.

EZIO PINZA, Metropolitan Opera Basso and Broadway Star, dies at 64.

♪ Los Angeles Celebrates Igor Stravinsky's 75th Birthday With The Premiere Of *Agon* And *Canticum Sacrum*.

♪ William Walton Composes *Concerto For Cello And Orchestra*.

♪ Carl Orff Composes *Comoedia de Christi Resurrectione*.

♪ Leonard Bernstein Named Musical Director Of The New York Philharmonic.

♪ Maria Callas Triumphs In Inaugural Concert At New Dallas State Fair Music Hall Opening With An Aria From Mozart's *The Abduction From The Seraglio*.

♪ Dmitry Shostakovich's *Piano Concerto* Performed In Moscow With Maxim Shostakovich The Guest Soloist.

Famed Cellist **Pablo Casals**, 80, marries his fourth wife, Martita Montañez, a 20-year old student from Puerto Rico.

OPERA PREMIERES

♪

Blood Wedding
Wolfgang Fortner
(Cologne)

Thyl de Flandre
Jacques Chailley
(Brussels)

Assassinio della Cathedrale
Ildebrando Pizetti
(Milan)

The Moon And Sixpence
John Gardener
(London)

The Turn Of The Screw
Benjamin Britten
(Stratford)

The Portrait
Hilding Rosenberg
(Stockholm)

Les Dialogues des Carmélites
Francis Poulenc
(Milan)

Die Harmonie der Welt
Paul Hindemith
(Munich)

Venus In Africa
George Antheil
(Denver)

One of the architectural wonders of the world, the Sydney Opera House, *opens, providing a world-class cultural center for theatre, opera and ballet in Australia.*

Ballet Premieres

Agon
Igor Stravinsky (Paris)

Stravinsky

The Israeli Philharmonic, comprised predominantly of refugees from the Nazis, moves to a new, permanent concert hall in Tel Aviv with **Leonard Bernstein** conducting the opening concert and **Isaac Stern** as guest violinist.

Aaron Copland composes *Piano Fantasy*.

Gian Carlo Menotti's Symphonic Poem *Apocalypse* is performed in Pittsburgh.

Gian Carlo Menotti

The Prince Of The Pagodas
Benjamin Britten

Square Dance
George Balanchine
New York City Ballet

Sebastian
Agnes de Mille
(An experimental piece performed without music, costumes or sets)

PULITZER PRIZE FOR MUSIC | Norman Dello Joio "Meditations On Ecclesiastes"

I Could Have Danced, Danced, Danced All Night

• **W**ith The Growing Popularity Of American Dance, American Ballet Theatre Sponsors Series Of Experimental Performances In New York.

• **N**ew York City Ballet's Prima Ballerina Maria Tallchief Returns After Brief Illness. Among The New Pieces Premiering Are:
  "PASTORALE" (Choreographic Debut By Francisco Moncion)
  "THE MASQUERS" (Todd Bolender)
  "THE UNICORN, THE GORGON AND THE MANTICORE" (Menotti, Choreographed By John Butler)

• **T**he Metropolitan Opera House Hosts The Ballet Russe De Monte Carlo In The Debut Of Several New Works Including "Harlequinade," "The Lady And The Unicorn" And "Sombreros."

Maria Tallchief

• **T**he Royal Ballet Visits The Metropolitan Opera House With The Incomparable Margot Fonteyn Dancing In "The Sleeping Beauty," "Swan Lake," "La Péri," "Birthday Offering" And "Petrouchka."

• **T**he Royal Ballet Flies To New York To Perform "Cinderella" On Television With Margot Fonteyn And Michael Somes Dancing The Lead Roles.

• **T**he Renowned Jacob's Pillow Dance Festival Celebrates Its 25th Birthday.

• **A**lwin Nikolais Stages "Runic Canto" And José Limon Produces "Blue Roses" Based On Tennessee Williams' "The Glass Menagerie" At The 10th American Dance Festival Held At Connecticut College.

• **J**osé Limon & Company Begin World Tour Under The Auspices Of The President's International Cultural Program.

DORIS DAY

JOHN RAITT

FIRE NOTICE:
route to the stree

Showplace

RADIO CITY MUSIC HALL
Rockefeller Center

Pajama Game *program featuring Radio*
City Music Hall Rockettes on cover

ON BROADWAY

CHITA RIVERA
& KEN LE ROY
IN LEONARD
BERNSTEIN &
STEPHEN
SONDHEIM'S
**WEST
SIDE
STORY,**
ALSO
FEATURING
CAROL
LAWRENCE
&
LARRY KERT.

ANOTHER OPENING, ANOTHER NIGHT

Robert
Preston
and
Barbara
Cook

THE MUSIC MAN

LOOK HOMEWARD, ANGEL

Jo Van Fleet, Anthony Perkins, Arthur Hill

THE DARK AT THE TOP OF THE STAIRS

Pat Hingle, Teresa Wright,
Eileen Heckart

ROOM AT THE TOP
By John Braine

ENDGAME
By Samuel Beckett

THE ENTERTAINER
By John Osborne

THE CAVE DWELLERS
By William Saroyan

THE WORLD OF SUSIE WONG
By Richard Mason

- **The Thrust Stage Is Introduced At The Stratford Festival Theatre**

- **Most Successful New Comedy: AUNTIE MAME With Rosalind Russell**

Most Successful New Musical: NEW GIRL IN TOWN Based On "Anna Christie"

- **Cost Of A Theatre Ticket: $ 1.15 - 4.50**

A VISIT TO A SMALL PLANET
By Gore Vidal

Eddie Mayehoff *(left)* and Cyril Ritchard

1957 Tony Awards

Outstanding Play
"Long Day's Journey Into Night"
Eugene O'Neill

Outstanding Musical
"My Fair Lady"
Alan Jay Lerner & Frederick Loewe

Outstanding Dramatic Actor
Fredric March
"Long Day's Journey Into Night"

Outstanding Dramatic Actress
Margaret Leighton
"Separate Tables"

Outstanding Musical Actor
Rex Harrison
"My Fair Lady"

Outstanding Musical Actress
Judy Holliday
"Bells Are Ringing" "My Fair Lady"

Outstanding Supporting or Featured Dramatic Actor
Frank Conroy
"The Potting Shed"

Outstanding Supporting or Featured Dramatic Actress
Peggy Cass
"Auntie Mame"

Outstanding Supporting or Featured Musical Actor
Sydney Chaplin
"Bells Are Ringing"

Outstanding Supporting or Featured Musical Actress
Edie Adams
"Li'l Abner"

Outstanding Director
Moss Hart
"My Fair Lady"

PASSINGS

Maria Pavona Chekhova, devoted sister of Russian Playwright Anton Chekhov, dies at 93.

Sir Laurence Olivier

Receives Honorary Doctor's Degree From Oxford University

Sir Laurence Olivier

And His Wife, Vivien Leigh, Lead Protest Against The Destruction Of London's Historic St. James Theatre.

EUGENE O'NEILL

Dominates The Theatrical Scene With Prizes And Plays Running On And Off-Broadway:

Pulitzer Prize
Long Day's Journey Into Night

Nobel Prize
Long Day's Journey Into Night
(Only American dramatist to have won this most coveted award)

Drama Critics' Circle Award
Long Day's Journey Into Night

On Broadway
A Moon For The Misbegotten

Off Broadway
The Iceman Cometh

O'Neill's Play, **A Touch Of The Poet** Scheduled For New York Production Next Year.

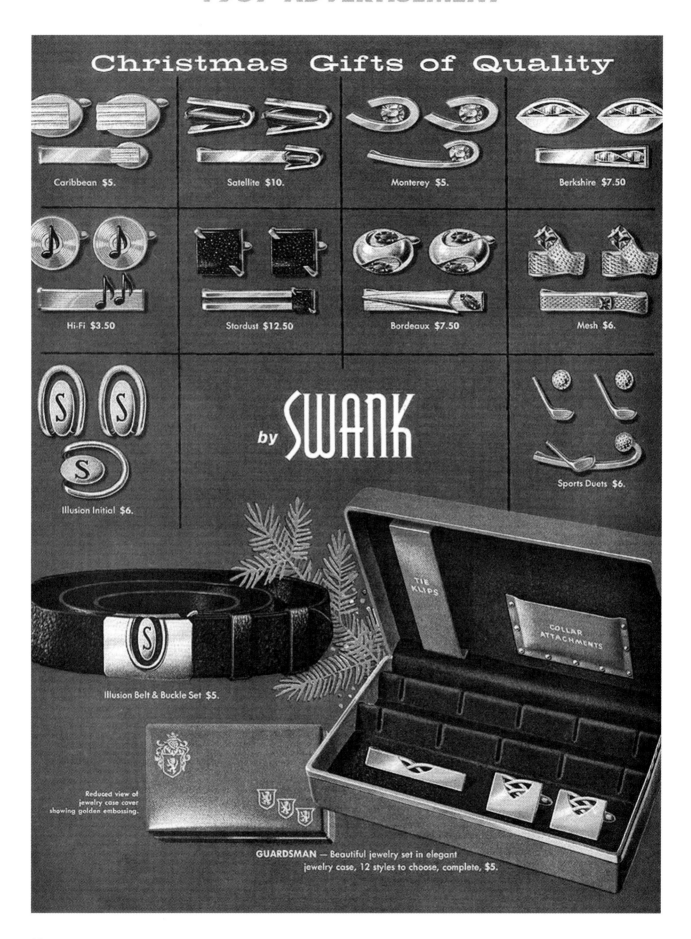

Christmas Gifts of Quality

Caribbean $5.

Satellite $10.

Monterey $5.

Berkshire $7.50

Hi-Fi $3.50

Stardust $12.50

Bordeaux $7.50

Mesh $6.

Illusion Initial $6.

by SWANK

Sports Duets $6.

Illusion Belt & Buckle Set $5.

Reduced view of jewelry case cover showing golden embossing.

TIE KLIPS

COLLAR ATTACHMENTS

GUARDSMAN — Beautiful jewelry set in elegant jewelry case, 12 styles to choose, complete, $5.

NEW WORKS OF NOTE

JEAN DUBUFFET
Mirandoliana painting

HENRY MOORE
Reclining Figure sculpture

PABLO PICASSO
Las Meninas painting

MARK TOBEY
Calligraphy In White painting

MARK ROTHKO
Black Over Reds, Red, White And Brown painting

ADOLPH GOTTLIEB
Blast I painting

WILLIAM BAZIOTES
Red Landscape painting

ROBERT RAUSCHENBERG
Painting With Red Letter 'S' painting

PHILIP GUSTON
The Clock, Painter's City painting

ANDREW WYETH
Brown Swiss painting

RICHARD DIEBENKORN
Girl Looking At Landscape painting

ELLSWORTH KELLY
New York, New York painting

HELEN FRANKENTHALER
Jacob's Ladder painting

The Brooklyn Museum holds a showing called *Religious Paintings*, including *Madonna And Child* by **Lorenzo Monaco** with other works by **Veneziano**, **Mantegna**, **Titian**, **Tiepolo**, **Rembrandt**, **Rubens**, **Delacroix** and **Degas**.

The Cleveland Museum of Art holds an exhibition called *The Venetian Tradition* including paintings, drawings and objects d'art dating from the early 16th century to the present day with artists such as **Rubens**, **Piazetti**, **Watteau**, **Delacroix**, **Renoir** and **Cezanne**.

THE LARGEST RARE PRINT EXHIBITION EVER ASSEMBLED IN THE UNITED STATES IS HELD AT THE MINNEAPOLIS INSTITUTE OF THE ARTS WHICH ALSO ARRANGES A LARGE ONE-MAN EXHIBITION OF THE WORK OF CLAUDE MONET IN COOPERATION WITH THE CITY ART MUSEUM OF ST. LOUIS.

GOING, GOING, GONE

Gaugin's *Still Life With Apples* sells for the highest price ever paid for modern art—$346,170—at a Paris gallery, with **Renoir**'s *Mosque in Algiers* and **Claude Monet**'s *Antibes from the Garden of Salis* selling for $73,228 and $53,650, respectively.

Sotheby Gallery holds London's biggest sale since 1928, auctioning off **Vincent Van Gogh**'s *Les Usines á Clichy* at $86,800 and his *Head of an Angel* For $72,800.

The Museum Of Primitive Art Sponsored By Nelson A. Rockefeller Opens In New York.

The Museum Of Modern Art mounts a one-man exhibition of JACKSON POLLOCK, the American Abstract Expressionist painter who died last year.

New York's Museum of Modern Art and the Art Institute of Chicago organize a **Picasso** 75th Anniversary Exhibition covering 60 years of the artist's work, including pieces from his own collection: *The Pipes Of Pan, Woman Dressing Her Hair, Paul As Harlequin, Portrait Of J.R. With Roses* and *Still Life With Chair Caning.*

An exhibition of the **Joseph Pulitzer, Jr.** Collection is held at the Fogg Museum in Cambridge and the Knoedler Galleries in New York for the benefit of Harvard University, including **Matisse**'s *The Bathers* and **Picasso**'s *Woman In Yellow.*

ART PRIZES

The Art Institute Of Chicago

Eleanor Coen "Growing City" (painting $1,500)
Robert Anderson "Yesterday, Today And Tomorrow" (collage $1,000)
Richard Hunt "Steel Bloom" (welded sculpture $750)

Pennsylvania Academy Of The Fine Arts

Henry C. Pitz Winner, The Philadelphia Watercolor Club Medal

The 4th Biennale At São Paulo, Brazil

Ben Nicholson Winner, First Prize For Painting (Also received Guggenheim Award of $10,000)

Art Institute Of Chicago's 62nd American Exhibition Of Painting And Sculpture

Seymour Lipton "The Cloak" (welded sculpture, First Prize: $2,000)
James Brooks "R-1953" (Abstract-Expressionism, Second Prize: $1,000)
Hedda Sterne "New York" (Abstract, Third Prize: $750)

Washington's 25th Biennial Exhibition Of Contemporary American Art At The Corcoran Gallery Of Art

Loren MacIver "The Street" (First Prize)
Fritz Glarner "Recreational Painting No. 79" (Second Prize)
Josef Albers "Homage To The Square" (Third Prize)

New York's Guggenheim Museum has exhibition of **Marcel Duchamp, Raymond Duchamp-Villon** and **Jacques Villon**, three influential French brothers active in the modern movement.

PASSINGS

FRANTISEK KUPKA, Czech painter who created first totally abstract work.

DIEGO RIVERA, controversial Mexican mural painter, dies at 71.

Rumanian sculptor CONSTANTIN BRANCUSI, known for the beautiful simplicity of his work, is dead at 81.

French artist **JEAN COCTEAU** designs the paintings, altar and all other decorations for a 14th-century chapel in Villefranche-sur-Mer, a French fishing village.

Books

Despite receiving many rejections from publishers because of the strange pictures and peculiar rhymes, Theodor Geisel — better known as **Dr. Seuss** — persists and gets a publishing deal for **The Cat In The Hat**, which appears to intrigue adults as much as the wee folks. **How The Grinch Stole Christmas** is also published.

●✧ The NEW CAMBRIDGE MODERN HISTORY Begins Publication.

●✧ JOHN DOS PASSOS Is Awarded The National Institute Of Arts And Letters Gold Medal For Fiction, Awarded Once Every Ten Years.

●✧ Farleigh Dickinson University Begins Publishing THE LITERARY REVIEW: AN INTERNATIONAL JOURNAL OF CONTEMPORARY WRITING.

●✧ 200,000 Copies Of FRANÇOISE SAGAN's Third Novel In Four Years, IN A MONTH, IN A YEAR Hits Paris Bookstores.

●✧ ALLEN GINSBERG's U.K.-printed poem HOWL is seized by U.S. customs officials on grounds of obscenity.

Jack Kerouac's stream-of consciousness novel *On The Road* gives rise to the words "Beat" and "Beatnik" as popular phrases to describe the "Beat Generation."

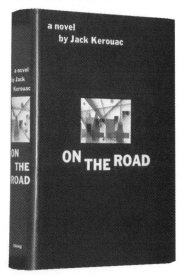

Books

James Agee
A DEATH IN THE FAMILY

Winston S. Churchill
A HISTORY OF THE
ENGLISH SPEAKING
PEOPLES, VOL. III THE AGE
OF REVOLUTION

Kathleen Winsor
AMERICA WITH LOVE

Bernard Malamud
THE ASSISTANT

Ayn Rand
ATLAS SHRUGGED

Edwin Way Teale
AUTUMN ACROSS AMERICA

Theodor Plievier
BERLIN

Henry Miller
BIG SUR AND THE
ORANGES OF HIERONYMUS
BOSCH

James Gould Cozzens
BY LOVE POSSESSED

Dr. Seuss
THE CAT IN THE HAT

Erskine Caldwell
CERTAIN WOMEN

Kathleen Kenyon
DIGGING UP JERICHO

Boris Pasternak
DR. ZHIVAGO

Leonard B. Meyer
EMOTION AND MEANING
IN MUSIC

Robert Bolt
THE FLOWERING CHERRY

Ian Fleming
FROM RUSSIA WITH LOVE

James Thurber
FURTHER FABLES FOR
OUR TIME

James Baldwin
GIOVANNI'S ROOM

Jonathan Griffin
THE HIDDEN KING

Vance Packard
THE HIDDEN PERSUADERS

Lawrence Durrell
JUSTINE

Art Linkletter
KIDS SAY THE DARNDEST
THINGS

Isak Dinesen
LAST TALES

Gerald Green
THE LAST ANGRY MAN

Roger Vailland
THE LAW

Pearl S. Buck
LETTER FROM PEKING

Stuart Gilbert, editor
LETTERS OF JAMES JOYCE

Fred Hoyle
MAN AND MATERIALISM

Simone de Beauvoir
THE MANDARINS

Kyle Onstott
MANDINGO

Mary McCarthy
MEMORIES OF A
CATHOLIC GIRLHOOD

Trevor Huddleston
NAUGHT FOR YOUR
COMFORT

T.S. Eliot
ON POETRY AND POETS

NOBEL

Literature:

ALBERT CAMUS
(FRANCE)

PULITZER

Poetry:

RICHARD WILBUR
Things Of This World

History:

GEORGE F. KENNAN
*Russia Leaves The
War*

Drama:

EUGENE O'NEILL
*Long Day's Journey
Into Night*

Journalism:

CHICAGO DAILY NEWS

National
Reporting:

JAMES RESTON
New York Times

International
Reporting:

RUSSELL JONES
United Press

Biography or
Autobiography:

JOHN F. KENNEDY
Profiles In Courage

Nevil Shute
ON THE BEACH

Jack Kerouac
ON THE ROAD

William Hollingsworth Whyte
THE ORGANIZATION MAN

Edgar Preston Richardson
PAINTING IN AMERICA

Cyril Northcote Parkinson
PARKINSON'S LAW AND
OTHER STUDIES IN
ADMINISTRATION

C. Day Lewis
PEGASUS

Jean Kerr
PLEASE DON'T EAT THE
DAISIES

A.J. Ayer
THE PROBLEM OF
KNOWLEDGE

Max Shulman
RALLY ROUND THE
FLAG, BOYS!

Theodore Draper
THE ROOTS OF
AMERICAN COMMUNISM

Iris Murdoch
THE SANDCASTLE

Saul Bellow
SEIZE THE DAY

John Steinbeck
THE SHORT REIGN OF
PIPPIN IV

Langston Hughes
SIMPLE STAKES A
CLAIM

Chaing Kai-Shek
SOVIET RUSSIA IN CHINA

Irving Wallace
THE SQUARE PEGS

Marshall W. Stearns
THE STORY OF JAZZ

Françoise Sagan
THOSE WITHOUT
SHADOWS

William Faulkner
THE TOWN

Arthur Bryant
THE TURN OF THE TIDE

Richard Hoggart
THE USES OF LITERACY

John Cheever
THE WAPSHOT
CHRONICLE

Robert Paul Smith
WHERE DID YOU GO?
OUT. WHAT DID YOU
DO? NOTHING.

William Saroyan
THE WHOLE VOYAGE
AND OTHER STORIES

James Thurber O
THE WONDERFUL

Richard Mason
THE WORLD OF SUSIE
WONG

Laura Ingalls Wilder, author of *Little House On The Prairie*, dies at 90.

John Van Druten, author of *I Remember Mama* and *I Am A Camera*, dies at 56.

Gabriela Mistral, Nobel Prize winning Chilean poet dies at 67.

Nikos Kazantzakis, Greek novelist who wrote *Zorba The Greek* and *The Last Temptation Of Christ*, dies at 74.

Again — it's one of New York's finest hotels — with new lobby, new Cafe Lounge, 1000 new "Rooms of Tomorrow", air-conditioning, TV. A new era opens at the famed Sheraton-McAlpin.

SHERATON the proudest name in **HOTELS**

In The News

*President **Dwight David Eisenhower** is inaugurated for a second term in a public ceremony on January 21, 1957.*

His inaugural speech is a plea for peace among all nations.

"...May the turbulence of our age yield to the true time of peace when men and nations shall share a life that honors the dignity of each..."

INAUGURATION JAN. 20, 1957

EISENHOWER

WASHINGTON, D. C.

Ike and Mamie attend post-inaugural festivities with children David and Julie.

Politics and World Events

Egyptian/Israeli Impasse Delays Opening of the Suez Canal

l-r: Humphrey, Dulles, Ike, Lodge

President Eisenhower, vacationing at the Georgia plantation of Secretary of the Treasury **George Humphrey**, calls an emergency meeting of his top advisors, including **Henry Cabot Lodge** and **John Foster Dulles**, to discuss the Mid-East crisis. At the heart of the problem is the Suez Canal, still closed as a result of damage and sunken ships following the 1956 Suez military intervention by the U.K., France and Israel opposing Egyptian President **Gamal Abdel Nasser**'s nationalization of the canal.

The President is apprised of the deteriorating situation by Secretary of State Dulles. The gravity of the Egyptian impasse causes him to cut short his winter holiday and return to Washington.

United Nations Undersecretary **Ralph Bunche** arrives in Gaza to monitor the situation.

Planeta Genova, a small Italian tanker is turned back by the Egyptians as it tries to make its way through the Canal.

The captain of the Italian tanker is told he cannot pass because supposedly the canal has not been cleared of a sunken vessel loaded with explosives.

The Suez Canal is Finally Cleared for Passage

The last obstacle in the Suez Canal, the tug *Edgar Bonett*, is raised near the midway point of the waterway.

U.S. **General Raymond A. Wheeler**, organizer and supervisor of the clearance operation in the Canal, climbing aboard ship.

Observing the salvage are General Wheeler, center left, and Undersecretary Bunche, center right.

Removal of the craft, scuttled five months ago by Egypt, clears the way for passage in the near future, although the questions of tolls and control have still not been resolved.

Nixon Visits Hungarian Refugee Camps in Austria

– SEEKS SPEEDIER AID FOR REFUGEES

Vice President **Richard Nixon** is welcomed by Austrian dignitaries on his inspection trip to Hungarian refugee centers.

His trip includes visits to all the major collection points where refugees await their final destination. 21,000 refugees are authorized to enter the United States, but Nixon is convinced the number should be increased.

Old and young, they have come to these refugee centers seeking freedom and to try to convince Nixon that America should expand its quota.

Nixon and Tracy Voorhees, head of the refugee program, arrive for a meeting with President Eisenhower after their trip to Austria.

Nixon gives Eisenhower a report on the results of his inspection trip. His recommendation is for more help.

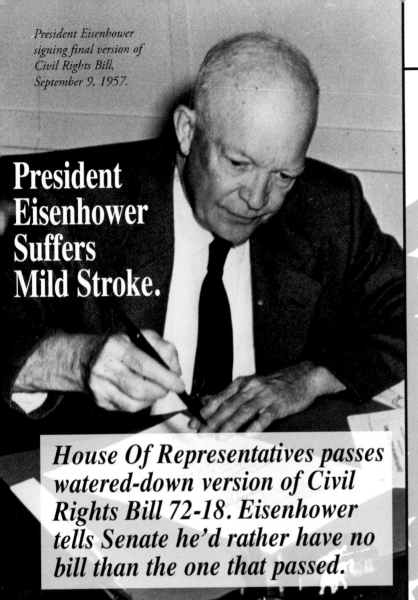

President Eisenhower signing final version of Civil Rights Bill, September 9, 1957.

President Eisenhower Suffers Mild Stroke.

House Of Representatives passes watered-down version of Civil Rights Bill 72-18. Eisenhower tells Senate he'd rather have no bill than the one that passed.

THE U.S. SUPREME COURT

...Upholds Ban On Sale Of Obscene Literature. Justices William O. Douglas And Hugo Black Cast Dissenting Votes.

...Rules That A License To Practice Law May Not Be Refused On The Grounds Of Past Association With The Communist Party.

U.S. MILITARY FORCE REDUCED BY 100,000 TROOPS BY SECRETARY OF DEFENSE WILSON.

U.S. State Department Refuses To Validate Eleanor Roosevelt's Passport For A Visit To Communist China.

Nine Democratic Women Hold Seats In The House Of Representatives.

Eisenhower Proposes International Arms Control

President Eisenhower Signs Niagra Power Bill Authorizing Construction Of Hydroelectric Dam.

Democrats Win Major Contests In Off-Year Elections.

Estes Kefauver Loses Foreign Relations Committee Seat To Senator John F. Kennedy.

Teamster Corruption Investigated By U.S. Senate.

James R. Hoffa

Teamster V.P. Jimmy Hoffa Arrested By FBI On Bribery Charges.

Jimmy Hoffa Indicted On Charges Of Bribery, Conspiracy And Obstruction Of Justice For Trying To Get Senate Committee Files.

Expelled AFL-CIO Head Dave Beck Charged With Income Tax Evasion.

Teamsters Union Expelled From AFL-CIO When Jimmy Hoffa, With The Full Backing Of The Union, Refuses To Purge The Union Of Criminals.

Jimmy Hoffa Acquitted On Bribery Charges.

New York Mayor Robert F. Wagner, Jr. Wins Re-Election By A Record Margin Of Over 919,000 Votes While Traditionally Republican Up-State New York Goes Democrat Electing Five New Mayors.

William Proxmire, The First Democrat To Be Elected To The U.S. Senate In The State Of Wisconsin In 25 Years, Wins The Seat Vacated By The Death Of Joseph R. McCarthy.

U.S. Communist Party Votes To Be Independent Of Soviet Control.

SOUTHERN DISCOMFORT

Interracial athletic events are outlawed by the Georgia State Legislature.

A bomb rips through a Nashville school that admits African Americans.

A black minister in Birmingham is beaten by a mob as he tries to enter a group of children, including his daughter, into an all-white school.

Willie James Edwards is forced by Klansmen to jump to his death from a railroad bridge in Montgomery.

> In 1954, the U.S. Supreme Court ruled in Brown vs. Topeka Board of Education that segregated schools are "inherently unequal."

THE LITTLE ROCK NINE

In September, nine black students—known as the "Little Rock Nine"—enroll at Little Rock, Arkansas' Central High School, touching off one of the key civil rights struggles of the decade. The students face violent protests from jeering, angry mobs of white students and adults, determined to block their entrance. Segregationist Governor Orval Faubus orders the Arkansas National Guard to bar the nine students from attending class. In response, President Eisenhower signs an emergency proclamation calling on all parties to cease and desist and dispatches the 101st Airborne Division to Little Rock to ensure the safe entry of the youngsters.

Despite a record filibuster lasting 24 hours and 18 minutes by South Carolina Senator **Strom Thurmond** (left), the first major civil rights bill since Reconstruction is passed by the Senate under the leadership of Democrat **Lyndon B. Johnson**. The bill not only assures voting rights for minorities, it also creates a Civil Rights Commission.

President Eisenhower and Arkansas Governor Faubus following a Sept. 14 meeting.

The "Little Rock Nine."

*U.S. troops escort the
students to school
in October.*

Russian Spy Arrested In Brooklyn

Vilyam Genrikhovich Fisher, a.k.a. **Rudolf Abel**, is arrested after a 9-year spying career for the Russians.

Fisher transported microfilm inside a phony coin container. The affair becomes known as the "Hollow Nickel Case."

Operating from an artist's studio just a stone's throw from the Federal Building, the Russian master spy will be tried in that very building.

1957

NEW AIR RECORDS SHRINK THE WORLD

This B-52 bomber flys around the world – a distance of 24,000 miles at an average speed of 520 m.p.h. – breaking all existing records.

CEYLON

MANILA

GUAM

CASABLANCA

CALIFORNIA
HAWAII

GEN. CURTIS LE MAY
Breaks Non-Stop Record

The jets fly 11,000 miles non-stop from Massachusetts to Buenos Aires in record time of 13 hours, 2 minutes, 51 seconds at a speed of 450 m.p.h.

General Curtis E. Le May getting ready to lead a group of jet Strato-Tankers.

PRIME MINISTER ANTHONY EDEN REPLACED BY HAROLD MACMILLAN

Macmillan

Britain's Prime Minister Anthony Eden's career ends after only 21 months in office, one of the shortest for a Prime Minister in Britain's history. The tragedy of the Suez invasion and ill health bring about his resignation.

Eden

Queen Elizabeth II replaces Eden with Harold Macmillan, leader of the right wing Conservative Party who will now have to face Britain's many financial problems and shrinking colonial empire. Son of an American mother, he will carry on the tradition of 10 Downing Street.

In an overwhelming vote of confidence, the Republic of Germany returns 81-year old Chancellor Konrad Adenauer (left) and his government to office.

Germany's Chancellor Adenauer Returned To Office

Enthusiastic well-wishers greet the Chancellor.

CANADA'S ELECTION UPSET

In Canada an upset election ousts Prime Minister Louis St. Laurent and his Liberal government ending his party's 22-year rule.

Winning by a narrow margin, newly installed Prime Minister Diefenbaker and his Conservative Party will be dealing with Canada's expanding economy and industry.

CRISIS IN JORDAN
MARTIAL LAW DECLARED
AS 6TH FLEET STANDS BY

A young soldier stands guard outside the palace.

The world focuses its attention on the royal palace in Amman, Jordan.

The young King Hussein, facing a political crisis as Jordan's Nasserite government maneuvers to abolish his monarchy, struggles to keep his nation intact. Failing to reach a political solution, he declares martial law.

Loyal Bedouin sheiks pledge their allegiance to Hussein.

Facing the first test of his Middle East doctrine, President Eisenhower proclaims Jordan's independence to be vital.

Implementing the doctrine, heavy elements of the 6th fleet are put to sea under sealed orders for a show of force.

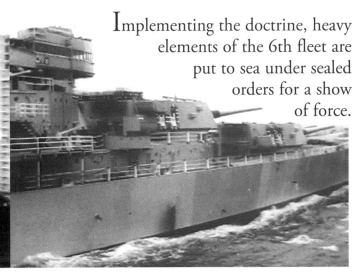

INDEPENDENCE DAY CELEBRATION IN GREECE

A NEW NATION IS BORN IN IN AFRICA

The King and Queen of Greece lead the parade celebrating Greek Independence Day.

Vice President and Mrs. Nixon are in Africa to attend ceremonies celebrating Ghana's independence from Britain.

The highlight of the parade is young Prince Constantine's first official appearance with his father.

Jubilant natives perform their tribal dance.

Greece's modern army presents a compact striking force. As a member of NATO, Greece occupies a strategic position in the Mediterranean during the present Mid-East unrest.

Nkrumah Kwame (r), pictured with Harlem Representative Adam Clayton Powell, is the first president of the former British Colony of the Gold Coast.

The 3rd Aga Khan, Mega-Millionaire Leader Of 40 Million Ismaili Shia Muslims, Dies At 80.

Mourners gather to pay tribute to their beloved leader, Sultan Mahommed Shah of Pakistan.

Before his death, the Aga Khan chose his 20-year old grandson, Karim Khan, to be his successor.

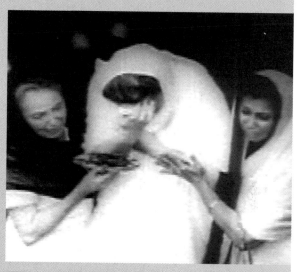

The Aga Khan's French wife mourns the loss of her husband.

Philippine President Ramón Magsaysay, Patriot And Leader Of His People, Dies In Plane Crash On Island Of Cebu. 2 Million Attend His Funeral.

Missile to Missile

First U.S. Civilian Atomic Power Plant Goes Into Operation In Shippingport, Pa.

The First Test Of An Atlas Intercontinental Missile Ends In Failure When It Explodes Shortly After Take-Off From Its Launching Site In Cape Canaveral, Florida.

James R. Killian, Jr. Named Special Aid For Space Technology By President Eisenhower.

U.S. Unveils Plan To Install Intermediate-Range Missiles In Western Europe.

U.S. Fails In Three Attempts To Fire Rocket 3,000 Miles Into Space.

U.S. Successfully Tests Intermediate-Range Ballistic Missile Jupiter.

U.S. Launches The U.S.S. Skate In Groton, Connecticut—Its Third Atomic Powered Submarine.

Navy Launches Rocket With Satellite Instruments 126 Miles Into Space.

THOR INTERMEDIATE-RANGE MISSILES TO BE PRODUCED BY AIR FORCE.

Nuclear Test Series Set Off In Yucca Flat, Nevada By U.S. Atomic Energy Commission Including First Underground Test.

The Soviet Union Launches *Sputnik*, The First Man-Made Satellite, Into Orbit Around The Earth. President Eisenhower Addresses Nation To Allay Fears Concerning The Soviet's Scientific Achievements.

In A Pact With The U.S., Soviets Agree To Place Earth Satellite And All Pilotless Missiles Under International Control. 22 Nations Support U.S. Plan To Limit Outer Space Exploration To Peaceful Purposes Only.

> The Army Air Defense Command Issues Report That New York And Other Major American Cities Will Be Defended By *Nike Hercules* Missiles With Atomic Warheads.

Soviets Launch LENIN, First Nuclear Ice-Breaker.

Asserting Soviet Missile Superiority, Khrushchev Challenges U.S. To Rocket-Range Shooting Match.

International Atomic Energy Agency Is Formed.

The Soviets Become The First Nation To Ratify International Atomic Energy Agency Charter.

Andrei Gromyko Replaces Dmitri T. Shepilov As Soviet Foreign Minister.

China's Chou En-lai Visits Moscow.

As A Warning To Western Europe Against Nuclear War, The Soviet Union Tests Another H-Bomb.

In A Move To Decentralize Russian Industry, Khrushchev Creates 92 Industrial Regions.

Soviets Agree To Western Plan For Atomic Test Ban.

Soviet Leader Khrushchev Promises Elevation Of Soviet Standard Of Living Stating: "Marxism-Leninism Will Taste Better With Butter."

Tito And Khrushchev Meet In Belgrade Pledging Closer Ties.

Two U.S. Diplomats Expelled From Moscow On Charges Of Spying.

Soviet War Hero Marshal Georgi Zhukov Stripped Of All Power.

First Russian Warships To Use The Suez Canal Since 1917 Pass Through The Waterway.

Members Of The Soviet U.N. Delegation Land At McGuire Air Force Base In New Jersey In First Soviet Civilian Plane To Touch Down In The United States.

CUBA & FIDEL CASTRO

Cuban Rebel Leader Fidel Castro Wages Fight Against Fulgencio Batista Regime From Secret Jungle Outpost.

Castro Interviewed On CBS Documentary On Cuban Revolution.

Cuba's President Batista Suspends All Constitutional Guarantees In Response To Outbreak Of Anti-Government Violence.

Castro Joined By Cuban Soldiers In Fighting South Of Havana.

Cuban President Batista Will Not Seek Re-Election.

INTERNATIONAL HEADLINES

Saudi Arabia's King Saud Visits Washington With Son On Official Visit.

Agreement Regulating Seal Hunting Ratified By The U.S., Soviet Union, Canada And Japan.

U.S. Continues Its Policy Of Non-Recognition Of Red China.

Benito Mussolini's Widow Receives Permission From The Italian Government To Exhume The Coffin Of Il Duce To Hold A Funeral.

François Duvalier Elected President Of Haiti.

French And British Banks Nationalized By Egypt.

Egypt Bars Israel Access To The Suez Canal And Saudi Arabia Cuts Off Gulf Of Aqaba.

Kashmir Becomes Indian State.

American Occupation Headquarters In Japan Is Dismantled.

The U.N. Demands Complete And Unconditional Israeli Withdrawal From The Gaza Strip. Thousands Of Israelis Protest.

Israel Withdraws From The Gaza Strip.

Indonesian President Sukarno Escapes Assassination Attempt In Jakarta.

Archbishop Makarios Is Released By The British Who Bar Him From Cyprus.

With U.S. Backing In The Form Of $10 Million In Foreign Aid, Jordan's King Hussein Leads Military Coup Ousting Pro-Egyptian Sympathizers In Government.

Israel Offers To Negotiate With Arabs On Refugee Problem.

Egypt, Saudi Arabia And Syria Sign Accord To Replace British Aid To Jordan.

Jordan Closes Embassy In Cairo.

Announcement From Jerusalem On The Fall Of Premier David Ben Gurion's Coalition Government.

A Grenade Attack Injures Israeli Premier David Ben-Gurion Along With Four Cabinet Members.

Hungary Institutes Death Penalty For Strikes And Other Acts Of Civil Disobedience.

Three Leaders Of The Hungarian Uprising Sentenced To Death.

Ireland Elects Eamon de Valera As Prime Minister.

French Government Tries To Restore Peace In Algiers.

GREAT BRITAIN

◆ QUEEN ELIZABETH II OPENS CANADIAN PARLIAMENT, THE FIRST REIGNING MONARCH TO DO SO. THEN ON TO THE U.S. FOR STATE FUNCTIONS INCLUDING VISIT TO WILLIAMSBURG, THE FIRST BRITISH SETTLEMENT.

◆ QUEEN ELIZABETH II ABOLISHES PRESENTATION AT COURT FOR DEBUTANTES.

◆ WOMEN TO SIT IN BRITAIN'S HOUSE OF LORDS FOR THE FIRST TIME IN HISTORY.

◆ MALAYA, THE LAST OF BRITAIN'S ASIAN COLONIES, WINS INDEPENDENCE AND ELECTS FIRST RULER, SIR ABDUL RAHMAN.

◆ PHILIP, DUKE OF EDINBURGH, BECOMES PRINCE OF THE UNITED KINGDOM IN AN ACT BY HIS WIFE, QUEEN ELIZABETH II.

◆ GREAT BRITAIN GRANTS AUTONOMY TO NIGERIA.

NOBEL PEACE PRIZE

Lester B. Pearson

Former Secretary of State for External Affairs of Canada; former President of the 7th Session of the United Nations General Assembly

Zagreb, Yugoslavia Is The Site Of One Of The First U.S. Style Supermarkets To Open In The Eastern Bloc.

BORN IN 1957

Princess Caroline Of Monaco & Caroline Kennedy

Wisconsin Senator Joseph McCarthy, dies At 48 of hepatitis aggravated by cirrhosis, his political career in ruins. McCarthy spearheaded the anti-communist crusade that leveled accusations of disloyalty against hundreds of Americans and which many decried as a baseless witch hunt.

King Haakon VII of Norway dies at 85, succeeded by his 54-year old son, Olaf V.

McCarthy

Your heart will be glad you came by DC-7

Whatever your reason for getting there sooner...

Take the **DC-7**__world's fastest airliner

With its top speed a remarkable 410 miles an hour, the DC-7 wings you with velvet swiftness across the oceans, across the continents—anywhere in the world!

There's unbeatable luxury and comfort, too. The spacious DC-7 cabin is pressurized, air conditioned, soundproofed and tastefully appointed to make your travel completely restful.

Next trip, get there *sooner*, more *comfortably*—by DC-7. See why *more* people and *more* airlines fly Douglas than all other airplanes *combined!*

DOUGLAS

BUILDERS OF THE DC-8 JETLINER

People

MARLON BRANDO makes a plea for contributions to the International Rescue Committee to aid Hungarian refugees.

"...Give more than you can afford so that the Hungarian people may be reassured that they are not alone..."

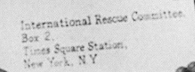

International Rescue Committee
Box 2.
Times Square Station,
New York. N.Y

Dublin's Jewish Mayor Visits Ike

Ireland's unofficial ambassador, Jewish Lord Mayor of Dublin **Robert Briscoe**, visits with Ike at the White House for an informal half hour.

Mayor Briscoe thanks Ike for the kind reception he received in America and for the gift of Irish cut glass—green of course.

THE MAD BOMBER IS CAUGHT AFTER A 15-YEAR BOMB SPREE

A fifteen-year reign of terror ends in New York when **George Metesky** is captured. The "Mad Bomber" admits to bombing 21 public places between 1940 and 1956 as revenge over being denied a disability pension. His activities caused a number of injuries. Found insane in April, he is committed to Matteawan State Hospital.

LIDO

Celebrities
Crowd Opening
of New Revue
at the
LIDO
in Paris

Salvador Dali

The Duke &
Duchess of
Windsor

Françoise
Sagan

Maurice
Chevalier

Yves Montand &
Simone Signoret

The Spicy New
Show is an
Instant Hit.

In the fabled Kingdom of Monaco, a new Princess has arrived.

The tiny Princess being held during the christening.

Princess Grace and Prince Ranier III, the proud parents, emerge from the church holding Caroline for her first public appearance.

In celebration of the birth of Princess Caroline, Prince Rainier III declares amnesty for all prisoners incarcerated for minor infractions.

In a bulletin from the Palace, Princess Grace of Monaco announces that, contrary to rumors, baby Princess Caroline does not suck her thumb or any other fingers and that she dislikes hats and having her picture taken.

Princess Grace

Crowds gather to celebrate the christening of Princess Caroline.

With another Royal arrival expected in March, everyone's rooting for a boy.

Queen Elizabeth & Prince Philip Visit America

Queen Elizabeth and Prince Philip are greeted at the White House by Ike and First Lady Mamie Eisenhower.

Wall Street rolls out the red carpet for the young Monarch with an extra special ticker tape parade.

Prince Philip chats with Mamie.

A water display in New York Harbor for the Queen's enjoyment.

A smiling Queen watches the waterworks.

Wall Streeters line the sidewalks to catch a glimpse of her royal face.

75

Queen Elizabeth Flies to Portugal to Scotch Rumors of a Royal Rift

Queen Elizabeth flies to Portugal to reunite with Prince Philip. The Duke of Edinburgh has been on a round-the-world trip and has been separated from the Queen for four months, the longest separation in their 10-year marriage, giving rise to speculations of domestic difficulties.

IS THIS ANY WAY TO TREAT A PRINCE?

Prince Charles, heir to the British throne, enters Cheam School, where he will share an unheated dorm with seven boys, sleep on a wooden springless bed, get caned for misconduct, and be limited to 35¢ a week spending money.

After studying a mountain of evidence including the testimony of anthropologists who compared her facial structure to photographs of the teenager, the 83rd Civil Chamber of the West Berlin District Court rules that ANNA ANDERSON is not ANASTASIA, the Romanov Princess who supposedly was the only member of the Royal Family to escape Bolshevik bullets, and has no legitimate claim to the late Russian Czar's fortune.

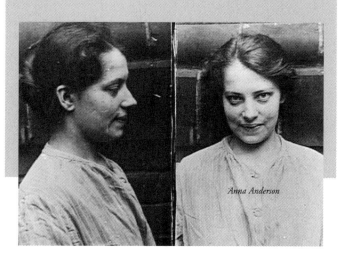

Anna Anderson

The glamour and excitement of New York's social season is enhanced by India's Mrs. Aga Khan (née Joan Lady Camrose) who arrives at the swank Waldorf Astoria to preside over a ball to raise funds for the Musician's Emergency Fund for hospitalized vets of the Musician's Union.

Gala Ball For Veterans

Mrs. Khan wears over one million dollars in diamonds at this most glittering social event of the season.

Unhappy with Graham Sutherland's portrait of her husband Winston, Lady Churchill puts a match to it with Winnie concurring that it makes him look half-witted.

Ernest Hemingway's dog, *Machakos,* is shot by Cuban soldiers searching for a rebel fugitive.

TIME MAGAZINE

MAN OF THE YEAR

NIKITA KHRUSHCHEV

WHAT A YEAR IT WAS!

AMERICA'S RICHEST MEN OR...
BUDDY, CAN YOU SPARE A MILLION?

Sid W. Richardson	$700 Million
J. Paul Getty	$700 Million
Arthur Vining Davis	$450 Million
Henry Ford II	$400 Million
Joseph Newton Pew Jr.	$350 Million
Howard Hughes	$350 Million
Clint Murchison	$300 Million
Paul Mellon	$250 Million
August A. Busch Jr.	$250 Million
John Davison Rockefeller III	$250 Million
Robert Winthrop Woodruff	$200 Million

AMERICA'S RICHEST WOMEN
LADY, CAN YOU SPARE A GIVENCHY?

MRS. HORACE DODGE, Sr.
DORIS DUKE
MRS. ALFRED DuPONT
MRS. EDSEL FORD
MRS. FREDERICK GUEST
MRS. CHAUNCEY McCORMICK
MRS. MERRIWEATHER POST
MRS. C.S. PAYSON
MRS. MARY G. ROEBLING
HELENA RUBINSTEIN

AMERICAN WOMEN PICK THE MOST INTERESTING MEN ALIVE

Sir Winston Churchill

John F. Kennedy

Bishop Fulton J. Sheen

Dag Hammarskjold

Henry Cabot Lodge, Jr.

Major Charles E. Yeager

Leonard Bernstein

Alfred Hitchcock

Paul Anderson

Peter Freuchen

Bobby Morrow

Frank Gifford

Mickey Mantle

Tab Hunter

Tony Trabet

Frank Sinatra

Albert Schweitzer

President Eisenhower

Edward R. Murrow

Toni Sailer

Dr. Harold Taylor

Roger Bannister

Pablo Picasso

Duke Of Edinburgh

Jose Greco

Harry Belafonte

Alfonso De Portago

Arthur Godfrey

Bing Crosby

Elvis Presley

Liberace

COUPLING

💙 Alan Alda & Arlene Weiss 💙 John Derek & Ursula Andress 💙 John Carradine & Doris Rich 💙 Bing Crosby & Kathryn Grant 💙 Linda Darnell & Merle Roy Robertson 💙 Anthony Franciosa & Shelley Winters 💙 Rex Harrison & Kay Kendall 💙 Howard Hughes & Jean Peters 💙 Jill Ireland & David McCallum 💙 Martin Landau & Barbara Bain 💙 Sophia Loren & Carlo Ponti 💙 Lee Remick & William Colleran 💙 Elizabeth Taylor & Michael Todd 💙 Francois Truffaut & Madeleine Morgenstern 💙 Robert Wagner & Natalie Wood 💙 Henry Fonda & Contessa Afdera Franchetti 💙 Susan Hayward & Floyd Eaton Chalkley 💙 T.S. Eliot & Esme Valerie Fletcher 💙 Lady Iris Mountbatten & Michael N. Bryan 💙 Harry Belafonte & Julie Robinson 💙 Don Larsen & Corrine Audrey Bress 💙 Marlon Brando & Anna Kashfi 💙 Nanette Fabray & Ranald MacDougall 💙 Lee J. Cobb & Mary Hirsch

UNCOUPLING

Elizabeth Taylor & Michael Wilding Lana Turner & Lex Barker George Sanders & Zsa Zsa Gabor David Lean & Ann Todd Brigitte Bardot & Roger Vadim Ginger Rogers & Jacques Bergerac Ingrid Bergman & Roberto Rosselini Gene Kelly & Betsy Blair Michael Caine & Patricia Baines Rex Harrison & Lilli Palmer Frank Sinatra & Ava Gardner Harry Belafonte & Frances Marguerite Byrd Belafonte Judy Holliday & David Oppenheim Frank Loesser & Mary Alice Loesser Aly Khan & Rita Hayworth Jack Webb & Dorothy Towne Edith Piaf & Jacques Pills

Guess Who's Not Going To Be Bringing Home The Bacon?

An Australian judge grants a woman a divorce on the grounds that on returning home early from her vacation, she found her husband in bed with another woman, who, mistaking her for the maid, ordered bacon and eggs.

DEAR ABBY

Pauline Phillips celebrates her first anniversary as Abby Van Buren, the fastest rising lonelyhearts columnist in the U.S. Syndicated in 80 papers, she is now ranked fourth after Dorothy Dix, Mary Haworth and sister, Ann Landers.

JACKIE GLEASON and his date are asked to leave Manhattan's swanky Stork Club because of their unruly behavior.

HEDY LAMARR QUITS HOLLYWOOD IN PROTEST OVER THE NON-CHALLENGING ROLES IN WHICH SHE IS CAST.

EARTHA KITT dines with Indian Prime Minister JAWAHARLAL NEHRU as part of her around-the-world quest for truth, meaning and knowledge.

Refusing to acknowledge Sophia Loren and Carlo Ponti's Mexican marriage by proxy, the Vatican attacks the couple, accusing them of living in sin and threatening excommunication.

Showgirl/actress Marie "The Body" McDonald's hysterical claim of being kidnapped, doped, raped and left in the California desert is thought to be a Hollywood stunt.

Sal Mineo tries a career as a Rock 'n' Roll Singer.

Abbott & Costello, broke and beset with tax problems, split up.

Bickering comedy duo Dean Martin and Jerry Lewis break up.

Colonel and veteran of 20 combat bomber missions over Germany in World War II, actor JAMES STEWART is nominated for promotion to Brigadier General.

In Memphis, **ELVIS PRESLEY reports for an army pre-induction exam in January, 1957. He receives his draft notice over the Christmas holidays.**

The Perfect 10 Face

The Caricaturists Society of America announces the perfect composite female face:

EYES:	**Elizabeth Taylor**	(Violet, Limpid)
FOREHEAD:	**Kim Novak**	(White, Smooth, Pure)
MOUTH:	**Anita Ekberg**	(Ripe, Sultry, Suggestive)
NOSE:	**Teresa Brewer**	(Cute, Slightly Turned Up)
HAIR:	**Sophia Loren**	(Silky, Soft)
CHIN:	**Natalie Wood**	(Firm, Round & Cute)
NECK:	**Barbara Ann Scott**	(Slender, Strong)
EYEBROWS:	**Maria Callas**	(Sulky, Passionate)
EARS:	**Helen Stevenson Meyner**	(Delicate, Small)

BODY CLINCHING OF A DIFFERENT KIND

Former Middleweight boxing champ JAKE LaMOTTA is convicted on charges of aiding and abetting a 14-year old prostitute to hustle "Johns" in his Miami bar.

Clare Booth Luce receives the University of Notre Dame's Laetare Medal for her brilliant career.

Serving a life sentence for killing his wife, Dr. Sam Sheppard is informed that a convict and drug addict named Donald Wedler has confessed to the brutal crime, but that police have discounted the confession.

In his unrelenting battle against smoking, well-known surgeon Alton Ochsner advocates legal prohibition of cigarettes if the number of lung cancer victims continues to increase at the current high rate.

10-Year Old Robert Strom Wins Record Sum Of $224,000 On TV's "The $64,000 Question."

PASSINGS

Grace Goodhue Coolidge, beloved First Lady during her husband **Calvin**'s presidency, dies at 78.

George "Bugs" Moran, survivor of the 1929 Valentine's Day Massacre, dies at 64 in Fort Leavenworth Federal Prison.

Notorious "Murder Inc." figure **Albert Anastasia** is gunned down in a New York barber shop at 55.

Albert Anastasia

Elliott Ness, organizer and leader of the "Untouchables," a squad of nine honest agents assigned to overthrow organized crime, including Al Capone's gang, dies at 54.

Frank Gannett, who built a news empire consisting of 22 papers, four radio stations and three TV stations, dies in New York at age 81.

Herbert Pulitzer, only surviving son of late editor Joseph Pulitzer, dies at 61.

YOU SICK?
No scents
in that!

Specially
for YOU

King-Size Birthday Card: ▶

Opens to a foot and a half of wishes for the biggest birthday ever. A Norcross exclusive, in your dealer's special rack. Price $1.00.   Shown is #100HB993.

◀ **Queen-Size Convalescent Card:**

Stands 12 inches high, for an extra measure of "Get Well" cheer. Look for this Norcross extra in its special rack at your dealer's. Price 50 cents. Shown is #50CN700.

ON YOUR BIRTHDAY

'Taint hydramatic or fluid drive......

SORRY TO HEAR THAT YOU ARE SICK

There's a message here for someone you know

There's someone you can make happier today by saying "I'm thinking of you." Your thoughts, warmly and sincerely expressed in Norcross greeting cards will make you dearer to those you care about.

Whether you say "Happy Birthday," "Get Well," "Congratulations," or just "Hello," Norcross greeting cards say what you want to say. See the beautiful selection —from 5¢ to $1.00—displayed at your Norcross dealer's. You'll be delighted with the many wishes, said in so many pleasing ways.

NORCROSS **N**
GREETING CARDS
Say the things you want to say

HAPPY BIRTHDAY!
Though you've had a few
Since your girl scout days....

Your Birthday

A Friendly Wish for GOOD HEALTH

How's tricks in your NEW HOME?

God's Greatest Gift

Bless the little one who's come
To make the world so sweet—

Some Get-Well Wishes

To BOTH OF YOU on Your Anniversary

©NORCROSS, INC.

Human Interest

Chefs participate
in the Culinary Arts
Show sponsored by the
Cooks and Pastry Cooks Union.

These most
talented chefs show off
their totally edible
creations.

PLATYPUSES COME TO AMERICA

New York's Bronx Zoo built a special tank to house three Platypuses sent from Australia – the only ones in captivity in the U.S.

A happy zookeeper gives a smiling welcome as he holds one of these odd little fellows.

In any case, these kids are having a great time with a new-found playmate.

The Platypus is a mammal that lays eggs, swims like a fish, looks like a beaver and is a puzzlement to scientists.

High school students in Houston, Texas practice Super Yo-Yo or Cheer-E-O, a revised form of yo-yo brought down from Canada by nine Canadian champs.

The Canadian visitors demonstrate the technical difference between the two pastimes.

Experts say that Cheer-E-O with its smoother axle and better balance is a top notch sporting device.

TEXAS YO-YO CRAZE

Claiming an endless array of tricks, the experts demonstrate some of the most popular ones including "The Magic Twirl."

The *New York Evening Enquirer* is renamed the *National Enquirer.*

SO MUCH FOR ROCK HUDSON & JOHN WAYNE

Oxford University's Union Society votes in favor of a motion to resist the influence of American culture on their way of life.

Colliers magazine and *Woman's Home Companion* cease publication.

Los Angeles revises its building codes, allowing construction of high-rise buildings using earthquake stress engineering.

Professor Reuben Hill of the Institute of Research in Social Sciences at the University of North Carolina claims that, despite the growing divorce rate and increased juvenile delinquency, the American family is not breaking up because the quality of interpersonal skills has vastly improved.

According to a Chicago psychologist, parents can keep their children from developing anti-social behavior by whispering loving words in their ears as they sleep.

Juvenile delinquency reaches epidemic proportions around the world.

Major crime in the U.S. rises by 7.5% according to Director of the F.B.I., J. Edgar Hoover.

The Harry S. Truman Library opens in Independence, Missouri.

A U.S. flag flies for the first time on Wilkes Land, Antarctica.

A 2,400-mile telephone cable linking California and Hawaii is placed in operation.

Construction of entrance channels and jetties begins in Marina del Rey, California.

I BET MY CAR'S BIGGER THAN YOUR CAR.

San Francisco State College semantics expert Dr. S. I. Hayakawa calls new cars symbols of the male sex.

ACCORDING TO METROPOLITAN LIFE INSURANCE COMPANY, AMERICAN FAMILIES ARE GETTING BIGGER, WITH COUPLES NOW HAVING A THIRD OR FOURTH CHILD.

• Detroit physician Dr. Albert D. Ruedemann, Jr. recommends that cars be equipped with front seat headrests to prevent neck injuries if a car is rear-ended.

In 58% of American families, wives either share or have a dominant role in handling the family finances.

The 6-lane Major Deegan Expressway opens in New York.

IF I WAS A RICH MAN...

Four out of five American men would continue to work even if they inherited a large sum of money.

Frank Lloyd Wright
Interviewed On "Mike Wallace Interviews" Show.

MAY YOUR NEXT HOUSE FALL DOWN ABOUT YOUR EARS!
Infuriated that one of his structures known as the Robie House is going to be torn down to build a dormitory for the Chicago Theological Seminary, 87-year old architect Frank Lloyd Wright declares that such destruction could only take place in America.

RIKERS ISLAND

27 prisoners in Rikers Island Penitentiary receive reduced sentences for heroic efforts in rescuing victims of an airplane crash during a blinding snowstorm.

Secretary of the Interior Fred A. Seaton designates 9,000,000 acres of land in the northeast portion of Alaska as a preserve for scientific wildlife studies and recreation.

59 nations participate in the U.S. Trade Fair in New York.

STRIKES

 A 36-day tugboat strike hits New York harbor.

Six major Boston newspapers go on strike.

◆ **The Supreme Court rules that First Amendment protection does not extend to obscene material.**

◆ **A New York judge releases Allen Ginsberg's "Howl" after the books are seized by police as obscene material.**

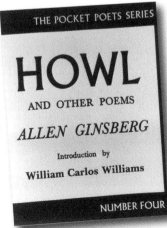

THE POCKET POETS SERIES

HOWL
AND OTHER POEMS
ALLEN GINSBERG
Introduction by
William Carlos Williams

NUMBER FOUR

THE POPE REDUCES TO THREE HOURS THE FASTING TIME BEFORE RECEIVING HOLY COMMUNION.

KENYA GETS ITS FIRST AFRICAN ROMAN CATHOLIC BISHOP.

Buddhist pilgrims converge on Katmandu, Nepal to celebrate the 2,500th anniversary of the death of Buddha.

SAY "I DO" OR DIE... SOONER THAN LATER

Statisticians of the Metropolitan Life Insurance Company report that married men live longer with death rates for single men 50% higher before age 45. The difference in mortality is not as dramatic between married and single women, however.

PASS THE BUTTER... I MEAN MARGARINE

Margarine exceeds butter for the first time in per capita consumption.

THE LADY IS NOT FOR BURNING

The 1692 witchcraft convictions of six Salem women are reversed by the Governor of Massachusetts.

They Don't Do Windows

Heirs to William Randolph Hearst's 120-acre unmanageable San Simeon estate, a repository for what might be described as an art collection bordering on maniacal megalomania, decide to turn it over to the State of California, with the proviso it be declared a historic monument and memorial to Hearst and his mother, Phoebe.

The U.S. Postmaster halts Saturday mail delivery until President Eisenhower signs a bill providing an additional $41,000,000 appropriation.

The Postmaster General establishes the Citizens Stamp Advisory Committee to evaluate the merits of new stamp proposals.

A visiting beekeeper at the Rio Claro Apiary in Africa accidentally releases 26 colonies headed by extremely aggressive African Queens.

75% of students polled by the New York Herald Tribune said they like school.

ANNUAL COLLEGE COSTS

Public College . . . . $1,500 Tuition & Living Expenses
Private . . . . $2,000 Tuition & Living Expenses

YALE UNIVERSITY RAISES ITS UNDERGRADUATE TUITION TO $2,000, THE THIRD INCREASE SINCE WORLD WAR II.

WE WON'T DO WINDOWS, DISHES, MAKE BEDS, VACUUM OR ANYTHING ELSE FOR THAT MATTER

While 8 out of 10 adolescent American girls want to grow up and be like their mothers, they definitely do not want to do housework and while 94% of young girls want to get married, only 3% would consider being full-time housewives.

Despite the decline in the number of fully qualified Geishas, the women are earning more money than ever, averaging $200 per month.

14,000 blacks and whites gather at Washington, D.C.'s Lincoln Memorial on a prayer pilgrimage for freedom, marking the third anniversary of the Supreme Court's desegregation decision.

"Gimme A Double Malted On The Rocks...With A Pretzel Stick"

According to a Yale Center of Alcohol Studies Report published in *The Journal of the American Medical Association*, alcoholism is virtually unknown among orthodox Jews due to the symbolic and sacred character of the use of alcohol. The orthodox Jew experiencing emotional problems would be more apt to work excessively, gamble or seek another outlet.

HOW DO I HATE THEE, LET ME COUNT THE WAYS...
Researchers at the University of California, Los Angeles, come up with the most common reasons for marital failure:
(1) Adolescent Behavior (2) Unconscious Anti-Marriage Feelings (3) Egocentric (4) Homosexual Tendency Or Male Passivity (5) Sexual Dissatisfaction & Projection (6) Rebellion Against Femininity (7) Flight Into Rejection

COPY THE CAT
President of the American Veterinary Radiology Society states that more and more dogs are developing ulcers due to the pressure of urban living – traffic, the barking dog next door, rough handling by children. The solution: copy the behavior of cats who are much more relaxed and don't get themselves upset over little things.

Asian Influenza
A Different Strain of Type A.

Crane Helicopter
A Helicopter Equipped with a Crane for Heavy Lifting.

Curtain-Wall School
A School with Movable Walls.

Blast-Down
A Rocket Ship Landing.

Bombardier
A Bomb-Shaped Vehicle Mounted on Skis for Snow Travel.

Borazon
A Synthetic Diamond-Like Substance.

Flying Seat
An Ejection Seat Designed by Lockheed.

Little Europe
The Six European Nations Comprising the Common Market: France, West Germany, Italy, Belgium, the Netherlands and Luxembourg

Calypsomania
Addiction to Calypso Music.

Mailster
A Three-Wheel Scooter for Mailman

Meter Maid
A Woman Attached to the Police Force to Write Tickets for Parking Meter Violations.

EXPRESSIONS

Rockabilly
A Combination of Country and Rock Sounds.

Stratospheric Drip
Fallout.

Subliminal Projection
Advertising Designed to Reach the Unconscious of the Viewers.

Scuba
Self-Contained Underwater Breathing Apparatus.

Skort
Combination Skirt and Shorts.

Teleprompted
Aided by a Teleprompter.

Total Theatre
A Theatre Piece which Utilizes All Aspects of the Performing Arts.

Space Biology
The Study of Effects of High Altitude on Humans.

Special
A Spectacular One-Off Television Show.

White Sidewall Haircut
A Haircut with Hair Clipped Short on the Sides.

93

New for Christmas! Twin-Cartridge fountain pen
holds 40% more ink...yet never goes near an ink bottle

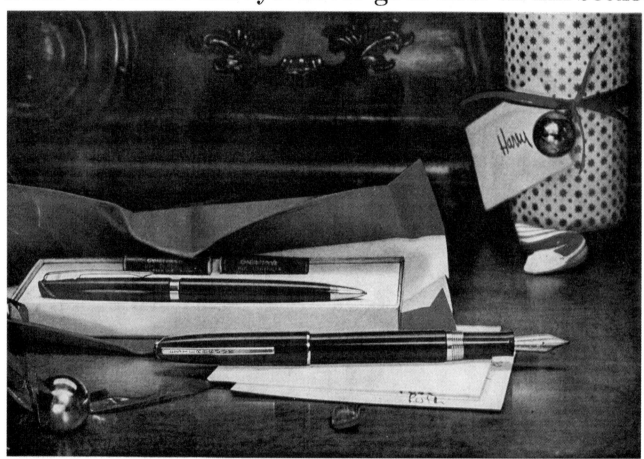

The beautiful new SAFARI pen and pencil are like no other writing set you ever saw before.

The SAFARI pen is a true fountain pen that loads with *two cartridges of liquid ink* ... never from an ink bottle. It holds 40% more ink than any other fountain pen ... yet is sleekly modern and slim.

You never run out of ink, either. The second cartridge is a spare ... always ready right in the pen. And only Esterbrook gives you a choice of 32 points ... replaceable in seconds at any pen counter.

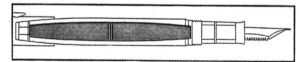

Two cartridges instead of one—so you always have a spare ink supply. Loading the SAFARI is so easy and clean, too. Just drop two ink cartridges into pen ... and you're ready to *write*. When one cartridge is used up, replace it ... and keep the other as your spare ink supply. You can buy economical packs of 6 big cartridges at any pen counter.

And the matching SAFARI pencil is completely unique, too. You feed *two feet of lead* without reloading—simply by pressing its push-top.

People expect Esterbrook's superb new SAFARI pen and pencil set to cost $25.00 or more. Guess again! The sensible price—complete with cartridges—is just $7.75. Pen alone only $3.95.

Esterbrook®
SAFARI*
TWIN-CARTRIDGE FOUNTAIN PEN
only $3.95

Only Esterbrook gives you a choice of 32 points—replaceable in seconds.

student   Signature Stub   bookkeeping   fine writing   shaded writing

*TRADEMARK

94

Disasters

HURRICANE AUDREY
Leaves Wake of Destruction In Her Path

Hurricane Audrey roars ashore near the Texas/Louisiana border on June 27, making a shambles of towns in her path. Winds as high as 96 m.p.h. cause storm surges of up to 12 feet, extending from Galveston, TX to Cocoderie, LA.

Audrey strikes without warning, leaving thousands homeless. 100,000 buildings are damaged, thousands destroyed. Cameron Parish is hardest hit, losing 90% of it's structures. Property damage is estimated at $120 million. Over 500 dead are scattered across a wide area and many days pass before the final death count can be estimated.

Curiously, on the evening before land-fall, masses of crawfish are observed fleeing the marshes in the vicinity.

BLIZZARD HITS THE MIDWEST

Hundreds of cars are marooned as a snowstorm blankets the south and midwest with drifts of up to 30 feet in some places and a death toll of 38 persons

A transcontinental train is completely buried with more than 200 passengers trapped for over 48 hours.

Soviet ship *Eshghabad* runs aground in the Caspian Sea, killing 270.

NUCLEAR FALLOUT

Radioactive material spreads throughout the countryside as fire breaks out in the Windscale Pile Nuclear Reactor north of Liverpool, England.

Kasli, USSR is the site of a chemical explosion in tanks containing nuclear waste, spewing radioactive material and forcing the evacuation of the area.

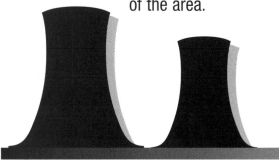

Northeast Airline's flight #823 crashes less than one minute after take-off from New York's La Guardia Field, killing 20 and injuring 50.

July: An earthquake hits northern Iran, killing 2,500.

December: An earthquake strikes western Iran, killing 2,000.

San Francisco is hit by its worst earthquake since 1906.

96

What's New

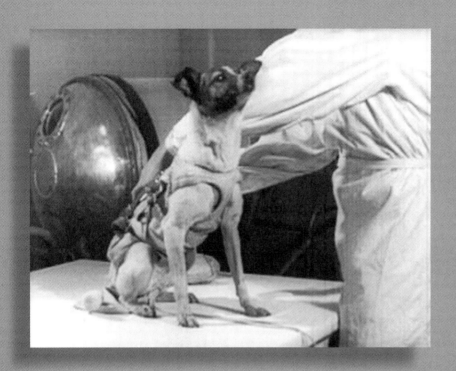

Laika, *a stray terrier from the streets of Moscow, becomes the first dog in space when she is launched into earth orbit aboard the Soviet spacecraft, Sputnik 2. Outfitted with a harness and placed in a padded enclosure allowing sufficient room to stand or lie, she is supplied with automatically dispensed food and water and monitored via a television camera. No provision is made for Laika's safe return and it is believed she perished after two days instead of the planned ten, due to high temperatures in the pressurized cabin.*

New Products & Inventions

Everyday consumer products have been given a new French twist, such as this stove in the shape of a snail.

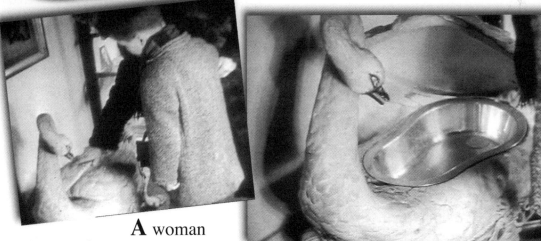

A woman with her son leans over to remove the cover from what looks like a swan.

Guess again. It's a wash basin.

And finally, two products that no French household should be without... knives with boots (left), and a cigarette holder with a tiny paper umbrella to keep the smoke out of your eyes.

The sphere above is a "core" for one kind of research atomic reactor. The metal tubes in the foreground and at the right show various test designs for holding the small uranium fuel pellets in other kinds of atomic reactors.

Strange new "tools" of atomic-electric power

These are some of the strange new "tools" used to produce, test, or experiment with atomic-electric power. They are among the things that will help bring electricity from the atom.

"Tools" like these are being used in developing several atomic-electric plants now under way. A number of electric light and power companies from many parts of the country are working with each other and with equipment manufacturers and the Atomic Energy Commission to develop the plants.

For more than 75 years, America's independent electric light and power companies have supplied more and more electricity to this growing nation. Today they produce more than any other single nation in the world. And they have helped develop ways to produce it more efficiently year after year. That's why you can expect electric companies to continue to do their part to advance the new science of producing electricity from the atom.

America's Independent Electric Light and Power Companies*

Company names on request through this magazine

The Toy Chest

101

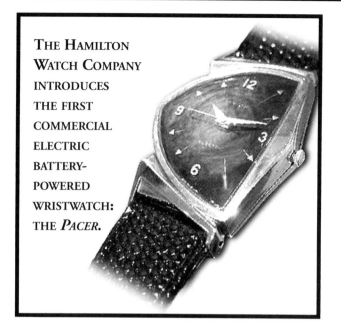

THE HAMILTON WATCH COMPANY INTRODUCES THE FIRST COMMERCIAL ELECTRIC BATTERY-POWERED WRISTWATCH: THE *PACER*.

A Copenhagen Yoga Instructor Designs Earth Shoes.

POCKET-SIZE RESUSCITATOR DEVELOPED FOR MEDICAL EMERGENCIES.

Earl Bakken of Medtronics, Inc., a Minneapolis-based company, develops the first external, battery-powered cardiac pacemaker.

The Delco Radio Division of General Motors develops an all-transistor car radio.

THE NEW "GENIE-LIFT-A-DOR," A RADIO-CONTROLLED GARAGE DOOR OPENER, IS DEVELOPED BY THE ALLIANCE MANUFACTURING COMPANY IN ALLIANCE, OHIO.

Brooklyn businessman Benjamin Eisendstadt develops *Sweet 'N' Low* with his son Marty, a chemist.

RALSTON PURINA introduces PURINA DOG CHOW.

1957 ADVERTISEMENT

for **easy-to-read copies**
the **first**
multi-purpose
photocopy duplicator!

copies literally anything on paper!

Anything written, drawn, typed or printed—in black or any color

Photographs or halftones

Opaque, transparent or colored paper with case or one or both sides

Heavy card stock that can't be bent or folded

Pages bound in a book or magazine

The new A. B. Dick photocopy duplicator Model 112 makes quick copies—jet black on bone white for easy reading—of anything written, drawn, typed or printed. Original can be on opaque, colored or transparent paper, or heavy board that can't be bent. It can even be a page bound in a magazine or book. No darkroom or special lighting needed. Easy 3-step process requires less than 5 minutes' instruction.

For more information about "the first multi-purpose photocopy duplicator" mail the coupon. Or visit your nearby distributor of A. B. Dick products. You will find his name listed under Duplicating Machines in the classified section of your phone book.

A·B·DICK
THE FIRST NAME IN DUPLICATING

A. B. DICK COMPANY, Dept. XG-57
5700 Touhy Avenue, Chicago 31, Illinois

Please tell us more about the new A. B. Dick Photocopy Duplicator Model 112.

NAME_____

ORGANIZATION_____

ADDRESS_____

An Automatic Air-Traffic Control System is Developed by Thomas M. Ferrill, Jr., Of Garden City, New York.

The General Dynamics Corp. develops the first electronic telephone.

Johnson's Wax Corp. introduces Glade, a home air freshener that claims to destroy odors instead of just masking them.

A water repellent for leather shoes is developed by Knomark Company of Brooklyn, New York which is said to protect shoes from rain for as long as six months.

The Frisbee and the Hula Hoop are introduced by Wham-O Manufacturing.

A shatterproof plastic window is developed by Seiberling Rubber Co. of Akron Ohio.

Flashing runway lights are ordered to be installed at Airports by C.A.A.

A miniature nuclear-powered battery with a 5-year life developed jointly by Elgin National Watch Co. and Walter Kidde Nuclear Laboratories.

B.F. GOODRICH CO. USES ATOMIC ENERGY FOR THE FIRST TIME TO VULCANIZE AUTOMOBILE TIRES.

A hot dog fork designed to roast six hot dogs at a time is introduced by Lockey Products, Chicago, Illinois.

Shatterproof, washable, chip-proof lampshades become available for the first time.

House of Vision reports the development of unbreakable lenses for plastic eyeglasses that are almost as scratch-proof as glass.

WHAM-O **FLYING SAUCER** REALLY FLIES 79¢
sail them straight or in a curve
— BOOMERANGS !

UNBREAKABLE! SOFT-SAFE

GENERAL MOTORS

The GM Golden Anniversary Chevrolet

The GM Golden Anniversary Pontiac

The GM Golden Anniversary Oldsmobile

GOLDEN FIVE for '58

PRESENTED HERE are five typical offerings of 1958 automobiles from our five car Divisions in celebration of the fiftieth year of General Motors.

They are automobiles that—to be worthy of this event—were dedicated to surpass their own traditions.

And, while each maintains its own personality, all five cars benefit — as does the public — from the combined ingenuity of their own engineering staffs and the styling, research, development and testing resources of General Motors.

From the General Motors Technical Center comes a steady flow of advanced engineering and design developments—basic betterments in transmissions and engines—new ideas in comfort and safety features—new concepts in styling and appointments.

It is this General Motors leadership which has created such outstanding values in the cars now ready for your inspection in the showrooms of GM dealers.

They offer you, we believe, the widest selection and the most satisfying motoring to be found today.

The GM Golden Anniversary Buick

The GM Golden Anniversary Cadillac

FROM THE PROGRESS OF THE PAST...THE PROMISE OF THE FUTURE

"Any cereal starts the day right ... as long as it's Post Bran Flakes"

LIFE IS SWELL WHEN YOU KEEP WELL ... like you do when you enjoy the "keep regular" benefits of Post 40% Bran Flakes. Tastes so good, too—lots of folks eat it for the flavor alone. That's probably why Post is the biggest-selling bran flakes in the world. Try some—see if you don't feel swell yourself!

"ALL POST CEREALS HAPPEN TO BE JUST A LITTLE BIT BETTER"

Post
40% BRAN FLAKES

Post

The Breakfast Foods of General Foods

SCIENCE & MEDICINE

International Geophysical Year opens with scientists and technicians representing 70 nations that will participate in an 18-month environmental study.

U.S. Air Force Major David G. Simons completes a record ascent of 19 miles in a pressurized balloon.

The first U. S. nuclear power reactor is dedicated by Army Secretary Wilbur Brucker at Ft. Belvoir, Virginia.

The first European particle accelerator opens in Geneva.

Micro computers are made possible through a new Cryotron device.

University of California's pioneering nuclear physicist **Ernest Orlando Lawrence** receives a $50,000 prize from the Atomic Energy Commission for his work in exploring the atom.

LEADING GERMAN PHYSICISTS ABANDON ALL NUCLEAR WEAPON-RELATED RESEARCH.

The largest radio telescope in the world is built at Jodrell Bank, England.

A prehistoric skull estimated to be about 45,000 years old is discovered in a cave in Iraq.

The physicist who helped develop the hydrogen bomb, **Edward Teller**, predicts Soviet scientists will be the best in the world by 1967 because of the high regard in which their people hold them vs. America, where scientists are thought of as squares.

The Journal of the American Medical Association reports that urban dwellers are safer from atomic fall-out than folks who live in the country.

THE HEART OF THE MATTER

Physicians at Philadelphia General Hospital develop a tiny microphone enabling scientists to study heart sounds and murmurs.

A new instrument called the Cardioscope allows inside views of the heart.

THE FLOWERS THAT BLOOM IN THE SPRING
(New Varieties)

CLIMBING QUEEN ELIZABETH:
Rose and Pale Pink Double Blossom Climbing Grandiflora.

JUNE BRIDE:
Creamy White Double Flowers With Moderate Fragrance.

GOLD CUP (Coupe d'Or)
Deep Golden Yellow Double Flowers With Moderate Fragrance.

Loyola University announces the development of a new powder food supplement which provides daily requirement of nutrients.

IBM makes the FORTRAN scientific programming language available to customers. It becomes the most widely used computer language for technical work.

MASSACHUSETTS INSTITUTE OF TECHNOLOGY ANNOUNCES THE DEVELOPMENT OF A SYNTHETIC PENICILLIN MADE FROM FERMENTED MOLDS.

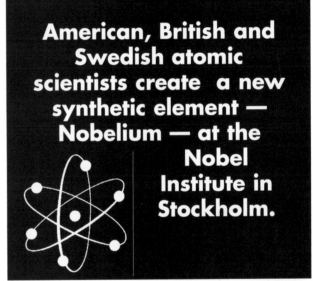

American, British and Swedish atomic scientists create a new synthetic element — Nobelium — at the Nobel Institute in Stockholm.

NOBEL PRIZES

MEDICINE & PHYSIOLOGY	PHYSICS	CHEMISTRY
Daniel Bovet (Italy)	Tsung-dao Lee (U.S.) Chen Ning Yang (U.S.)	Sir Alexander R. Todd (Britain)

The Space Race Heats Up As America Tries To Catch Up With The Soviets

America is shocked by the success of the Soviet space program, which includes launching tiny dog *Laika* into space aboard Sputnik 2.

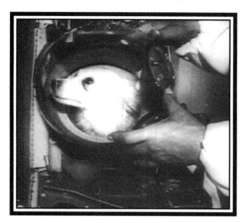

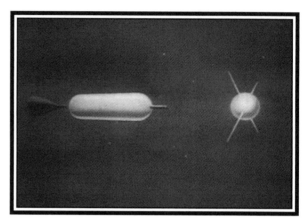

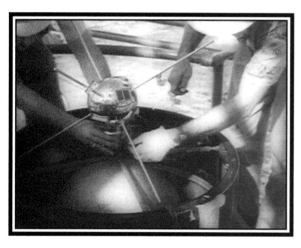

The U.S. tries to catch up by attempting to launch a grapefruit-size satellite on the Vanguard rocket. The results are disastrous as the rocket blows up two seconds after firing from its Cocoa Beach, Florida launch site.

Eisenhower Goes To Paris To Discuss Soviet Space Supremacy

In the shadow of Sputnik, President Eisenhower goes to Paris to meet with NATO leaders to discuss the Soviet threat. A decision is reached that three European nations will be armed with intermediate range missiles.

While in meetings, Ike receives word of the successful launch of the Atlas Intercontinental Ballistic Missile on a 500-mile flight from Cape Canaveral, which puts America in a position of beginning to challenge Russia's space supremacy.

MEDICINE

Surgeons find that, in cases of uncomplicated procedures, patients recover more quickly at home.

Breathing is more difficult for premature infants who are placed on their stomachs vs. their backs.

The American Medical Association releases a report from the American Cancer Society revealing a strong connection between cigarette smoking and deaths from lung cancer.

The U.S. Public Health Service takes an official anti-smoking position because of increasing evidence of the link between cigarette smoking and lung cancer.

Poetry used successfully as a healing aid in Philadelphia State Hospital.

- American Medical Association to study use of stimulants by athletes.

- Johns Hopkins University announces development of a vaccine against a major common cold virus developed by Winston H. Price.

- National Association of Chiropodists renamed American Podiatry Association.

- Air Force veterinarian Harry A. Gorman's all-metal device to replace hip joint in injured dogs used on a human victim of rheumatoid arthritis.

- Canadian psychiatrist names new neurosis: *Audiophilia:* excessive passion for hi-fi sound and equipment.

- **The sedative drug Thalidomide is released in Europe and Canada as over-the-counter Contergan. Widely used to counter morning sickness in pregnant women, it will be discovered to cause birth defects.**

- **Orinase, the first oral medication for diabetes, is introduced by Upjohn.**

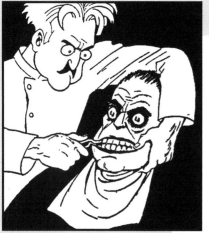

HERE'S SOMETHING TO CHEW ON

According to a report released by Seton Hall College, there is a definite link between personality and tooth decay. A person inclined to have bad teeth has characteristics something like these:
- Independent self-starters
- Welcomes responsibility
- Interested in intellectual pursuits

According to a study conducted by New York's Yeshiva University, men on skid row are just as intelligent as their non-skid row counterparts.

Surgeons enter the coronary arteries for the first time and remove fatty clots that lead to heart attacks.

Medical investigators report in The Journal of the American Medical Association that eating red meat before a football game does not improve a player's performance and that non-athletes live just as long as athletes.

Doctors warn that a husband should never donate blood to his wife because of the danger of RH-factor incompatibility.

OH MY ACHING HEAD

According to a study on headaches released by Louisiana State Hospital, recurring headaches are most prevalent in single women under 20 and people who are divorced or separated are more likely to have them than their married counterparts.

Photographed at the Blind Brook Polo Club, Purchase, N. Y.

THE SPORTS-CAR OF SPORTSMEN

Especially engineered to be driven by the man who lives for swift, sure-footed action in its fullest measure . . . *deliberately* styled to make him the envy of everyone else. Make a date for a test-drive today!

Austin-Healey
100-SIX

A product of The British Motor Corporation, Ltd., makers of
Austin-Healey, Austin, MG, Magnette, Morris and Riley cars
Represented in the United States by

hambro AUTOMOTIVE CORPORATION · 27 West 57th Street, New York 19, N.Y.
Sold and serviced by a nationwide network of distributors and dealers.

113

PROFILE OF THE JAYWALKER

- Potential Suicides
- Immature
- Personality Deviates
- Unconsciously Seeking Danger
- Or...Maybe Just In A Hurry To Get Somewhere

- Hypnosis is found to be an effective anesthetic during an operation.
- The World Health Organization develops a new technique for rabies protection by giving small doses of vaccine to potential victims.

According to psychology professor Dr. Cleo Dawson, women expect to be bossed and are more comfortable in that role than in the role of being bossy.

The Nobel Institute in Sweden develops a blood test that could determine if a person is mentally ill.

The use of forceps to aid delivery is thought to be responsible for 70% of Cerebral Palsy cases — Cesarean Section is seen as a safer alternative.

Chronically depressed mental patients stay that way because of their failure to see anything happy in their future.

The Journal of the American Medical Association publishes a report stating that tranquilizers can be injurious to mental health and can cause serious toxic reactions.

① #1 KILLER DISEASE IN THE UNITED STATES: HEART DISEASE.

WELL, I DON'T MIND IF I DO, SWEETIE, FOR MEDICINAL PURPOSES ONLY, OF COURSE!

A doctor at New York's St. Luke's Hospital recommends the moderate consuption of alcohol by older persons as an excellent way of improving the health of their mind and body.

THE CHEMICAL COMPOSITION OF TEARS IS THOUGHT TO BE ABLE TO DETERMINE THE STATE OF A PERSON'S HEALTH.

According to a study done at the University of Wisconsin, waking up tired morning after morning could indicate that you are anxious, tense, disinterested, bored or frustrated in reaching your life's goals and are unwilling to face your everyday problems.

Larger, more frequent feedings are said to ward off Colic in breast-fed babies.

PUT DOWN THAT HAMBURGER & FRENCH FRIES

The trend toward giving solid foods to infants is wrong according to a pediatrician who believes solids should be introduced around the same time as the baby gets his first teeth.

- Darvon is introduced as a pain killer.
- A one-minute test for Syphilis is developed.

The average age of lung cancer victims is around 61.

Smokers are more likely to give birth prematurely.

A study of 100 heart attack victims under age 40 reveals that stress is the primary trigger.

YOU ARE WHAT YOU EAT PERSONALITY PROFILE

Finicky	*Active & Impulsive*
Vegetable Lovers	*Work Alone On Theoretical Problems; Better Planner Than Administrator.*
Salad Lovers	*Outgoing, Social*
Starch Lovers	*Teamworker; Deals With Day To Day Problems; Good Administrator.*

- Two Philadelphia surgeons, Drs. Warren S. Reeses and Turgut N. Hamdi, successfully implant an artificial lens following a cataract operation.
- Baby pacifiers win favor with doctors once again as a means of preventing prolonged thumb-sucking and dental disfigurement.

A PIECE OF CHOCOLATE CAKE TO KEEP YOU WARM AT NIGHT

Soldiers fed a snack of between 600 and 1,200 calories before going to sleep in sub-zero temperatures woke up fewer times throughout the night and had less discomfort from the cold than those soldiers who did not have a snack. Who's got the pizza?

PASSINGS

BUT HONEY, BE REASONABLE, WHERE AM I GOING TO FIND COAL AT THIS TIME OF NIGHT — HOW ABOUT A PICKLE?

According to a nutrition survey of pregnant women, 187 out of 1,000 crave coal, while one wanted to eat the plaster off of her wall.

Admiral Richard Byrd, U.S. explorer, first to fly over the North and South Poles, dies at 69.

Joseph William Kennedy, one of the discoverers of Plutonium, the essential element of the atomic bomb, dies at 40.

So right for all the family—BLUE BELL clothes

You get so much for so little! Good looks, long wear—completely washable, sizes for everyone—98¢ to $4.98

Authentic western-cut Blue Bell Wrangler jeans, shirts, preferred by rodeo champions like Jim Shoulders. Sizes for all.

Fine for work or fun! Tapered Wrangler jeans in Sanforized denim; western-cut Wrangler shirt for dad. Frontier pants for sis.

Trim Blue Bell Jeanie pedal pushers and blouse for all the girls

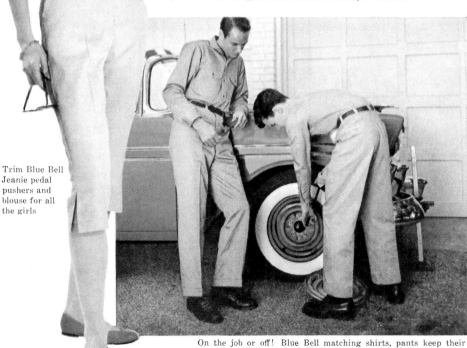

On the job or off! Blue Bell matching shirts, pants keep their neat looks long. Sanforized cotton twills; sizes for dad and son.

Blue Bell Jeanie shorts, blouses for mom, sis, too.

Look for this Blue Bell emblem—it's your unconditional guarantee of satisfaction

BLUE BELL

Blue Bell, Inc., Empire State Bldg., New York 1, N. Y.—Canada, W. Howick Mfg. Co., Montreal

It's a Living

ANNUAL SALARIES

Accountants	$ 6,000
Airline Pilots	$ 13,000
Financial Executives	$ 11,300
Dentists	$ 12,300
Lawyers	$ 10,200
Motion Picture Performer	$ 25,000
Physicians	$ 14,718
Psychologists	$ 8,000
Surgeons	$ 18,975
Teachers (High School & Elementary)	$ 5,000
Television Producers	$ 30,000
Television Performers	$ 10,000

Average Hourly Pay:
$ 2.10

**The Federal Hourly
Minimum Wage:**
$ 1.00

**Per Capita
Personal Income:**
$ 2,050

Illustrated above left to right: #6597 paper-wrapped, #6587 disc, #1207 woodcased.

Corrections are a snap with JOB-MATED ERASERS*

It's natural to make mistakes whether typing, drawing, writing with pencil or ink . . . on letterheads, carbon tissues, vellums or literally hundreds of kinds of paper.

Now, once and for all, you can forget those human errors. *Change your mind as often as you like.* Because Eberhard Faber

makes a job-mated eraser° for every purpose and every paper. Try one today—at better stores everywhere.

SINCE 1849 **EBERHARD FABER** WILKES-BARRE, PA. TORONTO

Erasers Easily Eliminate Errors

°*Mated to the paper type and designed for the erasure job*

Trademarks Reg. U. S. Pat. Off.

Pink Pearl "100" . . . Rubkleen "6002" . . . Ruby "112" . . . Star Plastic Cleaner . . . Specify choice of eraser on your company letterhead for free sample

AMERICA'S FIRST COMMERCIAL JET TAKES TO THE SKIES

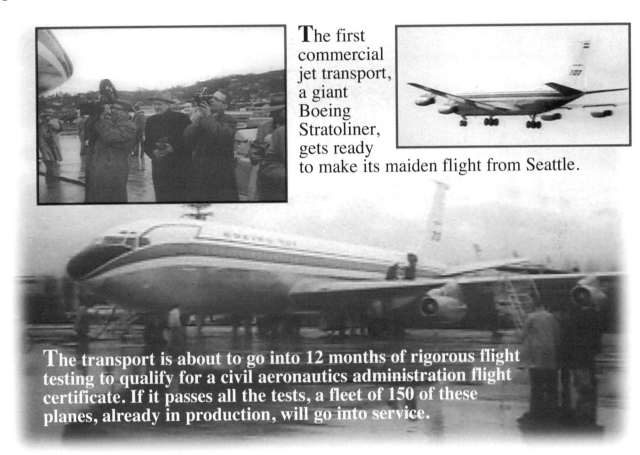

The first commercial jet transport, a giant Boeing Stratoliner, gets ready to make its maiden flight from Seattle.

The transport is about to go into 12 months of rigorous flight testing to qualify for a civil aeronautics administration flight certificate. If it passes all the tests, a fleet of 150 of these planes, already in production, will go into service.

DIGITAL Equipment Corporation Is Founded

PASSINGS

Diamond king SIR ERNEST OPPENHEIMER, owner of the De Beers Mines and controller of 95% of the world's diamond products, dies at age 77 in Johannesburg.

Automobile pioneer LOUIS SEMPLE CLARKE, who built his first car in 1896, dies at age 90.

Proctor & Gamble Acquire Charmin Paper Mills And Clorox

THE PRICE THAT WAS

Baseball	2.77
Bath Towel	.74
Coca-Cola	.05
Iron, Electric	.27
Flashlight Battery	.14
Diapers, Fleece	2.69

Aspirin (100 ct.)	$ .49
Baby Powder (4 oz.)	.49
Bath Salts	2.50
Billfold, Ladies	5.00
Blistex Lip Medication	.39
Box Spring	49.50
Candelabra, Sterling Silver	.155.00
Candy (Lifesavers)	.05

China, Cup & Saucer Set	$3.50
Cigarette Lighter	.17
Cigar	.10
Clearasil Acne Medication	.69
Clothes Dryer	199.95
Cold Medicine	1.00
Cologne & Dusting Powder Set	3.00
Cooking Pot & Cover, Stainless Steel (2 pcs.)	5.99
Cough Syrup	.39
Curtains & Valance	.97
Dental Cream	.65
Deodorant (Cream)	.43
Electric Shaver	14.95
Ex-Lax Laxative	.79
Eye Shadow Stick	1.00

Eyebrow Pencil, Automatic	$ .79
Eyelash Curler	1.00
Hair Tonic	.49
Home Permanent, Toni	2.29
Lamps, Boudoir	1.47
Lighter Fuel (8 oz.)	.49
Lipstick	1.10
LIFE Magazine	.25
LIFE Magazine, 1-yr subscription	6.75
Make-Up (Liquid)	1.50
Mascara	1.25
Mattress	49.50
Mixed Nuts	2.00
Nail Polish	.75
Pan, Frying (Electric)	22.95
Percolator (Automatic)	16.95
Rain Boots	2.00

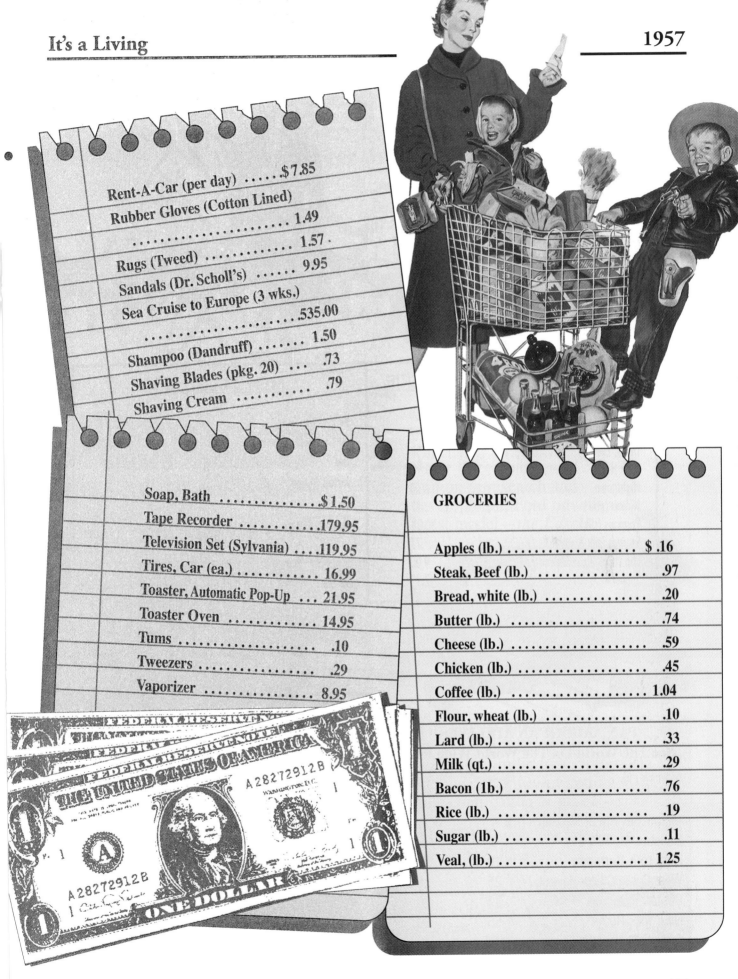

Rent-A-Car (per day) $7.85

Rubber Gloves (Cotton Lined)
.... 1.49

Rugs (Tweed) .... 1.57 .

Sandals (Dr. Scholl's) 9.95

Sea Cruise to Europe (3 wks.)
.... 535.00

Shampoo (Dandruff) 1.50

Shaving Blades (pkg. 20) ... .73

Shaving Cream .... .79

Soap, Bath $1.50

Tape Recorder 179.95

Television Set (Sylvania) ... 119.95

Tires, Car (ea.) 16.99

Toaster, Automatic Pop-Up ... 21.95

Toaster Oven 14.95

Tums .... .10

Tweezers .... .29

Vaporizer 8.95

GROCERIES

Apples (lb.) .... $ .16

Steak, Beef (lb.) .... .97

Bread, white (lb.) .... .20

Butter (lb.) .... .74

Cheese (lb.) .... .59

Chicken (lb.) .... .45

Coffee (lb.) 1.04

Flour, wheat (lb.) .... .10

Lard (lb.) .... .33

Milk (qt.) .... .29

Bacon (1b.) .... .76

Rice (lb.) .... .19

Sugar (lb.) .... .11

Veal, (lb.) 1.25

124

EUROPEAN COMMON MARKET TREATY SIGNED IN ROME

Rome City Hall is the site where an historic event is about to take place.

Long a dream, the European Common Market takes its first step forward as representatives from six European nations gather to eradicate customs barriers.

German Chancellor Adenauer, one of the chief statesmen at the conference, leads the discussions.

Belgium's representative signs the treaty, the first of several which are expected to unify Western Europe economically within the next 15 years.

With abolition of tariff barriers and the industrial integration of these nations, a new chapter is opened, economically uniting former enemies.

You'll feel a very special kind of pride the day you park a new Chevrolet in your driveway. Maybe you'll even find yourself looking out the window, now and then, just for the pleasure of seeing it there. It's a beautiful sight to behold—fresh and alert, with a certain ready-to-go spirit written all over it.

And when the neighbors drop by to "look 'er over," you'll be prouder than ever. They'll see fine construction and finishing touches everywhere. They'll feel the extra solidity of Body by Fisher, and they'll see the deeper luster of Chevy's *lacquer* paint job.

Then they'll want a ride around the block to see if Chevrolet is as sweet, smooth and sassy as it looks. That's how people become happy Chevy owners. Stop by your Chevrolet dealer's and you'll see what we mean. . . . Chevrolet Division of General Motors, Detroit 2, Mich.

More people drive Chevrolets than any other car.

You get more
to be proud of in a Chevy!

More beautifully built and shows it—the Bel Air Sport Coupe with Body by Fisher.

Fashion

The 1956 film *And God Created Woman* hits American screens. The vision of a bikini-clad **Brigitte Bardot**, heats up demands for skimpier swimsuits.

Fashion

COCO
CHANEL

The accolades pour in for Chanel, now a vital 71. Neiman-Marcus honors her with its Golden Anniversary Award for her enduring fashion contributions and for her ever-popular perfume, **Chanel No. 5**. *Life* magazine's August 19 issue carries a tribute to Chanel titled "Just a Simple Little Dressmaker."

Chanel, circa 1930

Variations on her famous two-piece knit jersey '20s suits are still in great demand and she remains an influencial marker for the young turks of couture. A tireless innovator, she introduces her new chain-handled quilted leather handbags – an instant success!

DESIGNERS MAKE

THE FRENCH | Ten years after the dominating influence of **Dior**'s "New Look" in the fashion world, the Chemise or "The Sack" is introduced by French designers **Givenchy** and **Balenciaga**. Shaped like a giant almond with sleeves, and obscuring the silhouette, American women complain that the Sack dress is hard to iron while American men complain about the lack of sensuousness. Regardless of the objections, the Sack influences designers, even in America. So much so that in March, *Time* magazine features the undisputed giant of fashion, Dior, on its cover. The accompanying story states that Paris designers like Givenchy and and Balenciaga will change the shape of clothing everywhere.

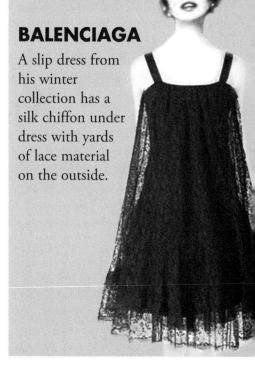

BALENCIAGA

A slip dress from his winter collection has a silk chiffon under dress with yards of lace material on the outside.

HUBERT GIVENCHY

Launches his Paris collection to unveil his "Sack," launching the trend for straight shift dresses which anticipate the loose and short look to come.

Italian film director Federico Fellini is enchanted by the changes in women's clothing—especially the sack dress that elemenated women's curves. "One day," he says, "I saw women walking along dressed in a fantastic and extraordinary way, so fascinating that it set light to my imagination."

Pierre Cardin Unveils His First Complete Collection.

PASSING

CHRISTIAN DIOR

The creator of the revolutionary "New Look," and recipient of France's Legion Of Honor decoration for breathing new life into France's fashion industry, dies at 52.

THEIR MARK...

The black silk polka-dot dress below, with bubble skirt and soft tie at the neck, can be worn with a matching white wool cardigan.

THE AMERICANS | Over the objections of American women and men who feel the "Sack" dress lacks sensuality, American designers fall in step with the Parisians, though somewhat downplaying the French *shapelessness*. **Luis Estevez** combines the straightness of sack with a lavish overdress of veil material. Free-form takes over some design with the look of ballooning skirts and bubble dresses. American designers are comfortable with the silhouette in various forms: **Claire McCardell** creates a "string bean" silhouette with a dress-length cashmere pull-over sweater. **Norman Norell** offers a beltless chemise and tubular tunic.

Basic sheath dress shown in black jersey (above left) and bubble skirt dress (top right).

fashion trendsfashion trendsfashion trends

for the GUYS

Styles range from the clean-scrubbed Pat Boone preppy look to beatnik chic consisting of khaki pants, sweater and sandals. Sales of blue jeans skyrocket – especially to teenagers of both genders.

for the Girls

Light, loosely-woven fabrics with bold patterns in deep red, orange, yellow, cobalt blue and green are the most popular colors, with shades of brown competing with black for evening wear. Sharp pointed toes and medium high heels highlight fancy dress shoes.

Stars and socialites model fashions unveiled at recent charity ball at the Palm Beach Estate of Mrs. Horace Dodge, II

Lesley Cunningham wears a romantic bouffant dress of white organza.

A picture hat completes the ensemble.

A floppy hat to keep the sun off her oh-so-delicate face.

The hostess models this beautiful organza ball gown.

Rita Moreno's strapless gown with a matching coat has a Grecian motif and is quite stunning.

Ann Miller looks smashing in her silk gown printed with huge blossoms, the back plunging to the waist.

The Three-Piece Ensemble

The look of the ultimate high fashion ensemble becomes available in various price ranges. The three-piece look offers dress-jacket combinations with slim-to-generous collars.

Moss green jersey dress with matching cropped jacket. ($69.95)

Sapphire blue tweed suit with straight-cut jacket ($47.00 shown with a matching blue silk blouse. ($10.00

Red tweed suit with matching handbag and beret.

A bright red knitted wool suit with a printed silk blouse in shades of red and gold.

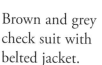

Brown and grey check suit with belted jacket.

Fashion

Deep red dress with matching jacket.

Straight black tweed jacket with sable collar, slim skirt.

Two-piece light pink wool crepe dress with pleated skirt and overblouse softly cinched at the waist.

Basic black wool suit, slim skirt, lightly fitted jacket and off-the-neck collar.

Light blue silk coat worn just above the knees sweeps backward into a light flair.

1957 ADVERTISEMENTS

ALL NEW

The only standard typewriter

with lig Golde

up to 26% LESS TYPING E

STOP pound-pounding away half your strength every day!

Lightest touch in standard typewriter history... brings you easy tap-tap typing! The totally new Underwood "Touch-Master" ends back-breaking, pound-pound typing forever! Just a light tap-tap puts those Golden-Touch keys into action. Immediately you'll feel the wonderful difference!

For a Golden-Touch demonstration, call your Underwood Showroom— listed in the Yellow Pages.

Magic Ex
Extra-easy
does it!
Extra-sma
Extra-clea
Touch.
Extra-sma
Beach Beig
Underwoo

Like wearin
Golden

underwood *only standard typewriter with Golden-Touch*

Japanese Ladies' shirtwaist, skirt cut in pleats and gores, in finest cotton. Fabric and dress designed by Constance Howarth, one of the world's top ten designers — and a Lancashire gir

EXCLUSIVE IN BOLTON
TO

Dorothy Dearnaley

FIFTY-EIGHT NEWPORT STREET, BOLTON
TELEPHONE 2009
AGENT FOR **WETHERALL** BOND STREET SPORTSCLOTHES

SALE $1.57 EA.

STURDY TWEED RUGS

SAVE 41¢ Take 'em home for every room. You can't afford to miss this bargain. Cut pile tweed rugs of viscose and acetate. Latex back; fringed ends. 25" x 37". Gold, Aqua, Red, Green, Pink, Grey. Reg. $1.98 each.

SALE 2 FOR 97¢

LUXURIOUS CANNON BATH TOWELS

SAVE 41¢ Just try to match this terrific value anywhere. Fluffy, thick bath towels 22" x 44" in Cannon solid pastels or smart stripes. Regularly 69¢ ea.

SALE 97¢ COMPLETE

CAFE CURTAINS & VALANCE

SAVE 52¢ Brighten up the house with the newest curtain fashion at a great savings! Smooth cotton broadcloth. 50" over-all width x 36" length. Valance 70" x 8" included. Latest designs. Red, Pink, Gold. Regularly $1.49 pair.

Shoppers!
Make SMASHING Savings

10 DAYS ONLY
Wednesday, January 9th, through Saturday, January 19th

on these eleven outstanding values
WOOLWORTH'S
January
$UPER-$ALE
Better hurry — they'll go like magic

...and all through January — storewide savings during Woolworth's month-long

97¢ SALE

Listen
To
The
WOOLWORTH H

Every Sunday afte
Percy Faith, his O
and Chorus, with o
ing guest stars, broa
"The Best in Music
full hour, live fro
York, over the CB
network.

136

SALE $1⁴⁷ EA.

BEAUTIFUL 14" BOUDOIR LAMPS

SAVE 51¢ Amazing lamp value. Get 'em for every bedroom. Lamps with matching shades. White glass or gleaming brass color base. Regularly $1.98 each.

SALE 2 FOR 97¢
Plus tax

FABULOUS COSTUME JEWELRY

SAVE 21¢ Smashing value in jewelry for every occasion! Top-fashion necklaces, bracelets, earrings, brooches. Sparkling simulated jewels, rhinestones, gold color, silvery metals. These'll go fast, so don't wait! Reg. 59¢ ea.

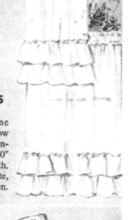

SALE
97¢ PR.

DOUBLE RUFFLE DACRON CURTAINS

SAVE 52¢ Imagine Dacron at this low, low price! Dress up your windows with tier curtains. 60" over-all width x 36" length. Lovely fresh colors: White, Yellow, Pink or Green. Regularly $1.49 pair.

SALE 2 FOR 77¢

LARGE SILK AND RAYON SCARVES

SAVE 35% Get armfuls! It's your chance to own imported silk scarves without paying fabulous prices. Large 33" x 33" size in exciting colors. Gay prints. Regularly 59¢ each.

SALE 2 PR. FOR 87¢

FIRST QUALITY NYLONS

SAVE 31¢ Buy a supply! Exquisite full-fashioned nylons at a next-to-nothing price. Hurry in, they'll go fast! Newest fashion shades in 51 gauge, 15 denier. Sizes 9 to 10½. Reg. 59¢ pr.

SALE 4 FOR 97¢

LADIES' FAVORITE BRIEFS

SAVE 38% Terrific reduction. Buy dozens! Full-cut acetate briefs; popular year round. With purchase of 4 save 59¢. White only. Sizes 5, 6, 7, 8. Regularly 39¢ pair.

Remember, there's also a storewide

97¢ SALE

going on for the whole month of January! Watch for 97¢ specials at Woolworth's all month long! (The 11 articles shown here are on sale only from Wednesday, Jan. 9th through Saturday, Jan. 19th.)

SALE 3 PR. FOR 87¢

MEN'S NYLON S-T-R-E-T-C-H SOCKS

SAVE 28¢ Buy 'em by the dozen for every man in the house! 100% nylon ribbed socks. One size fits sizes 10 to 13. Navy Blue, Brown, Charcoal, Black or Grey. Reg. 3 pr. for $1.15.

SALE 17¢ COMPLETE

IMPORTED CHINA CUP AND SAUCER

SAVE 37% At this low price you'll want a dozen of these beautifully delicate, expensive-looking china cups and saucers. Two shapes, three designs. Moss Rose, Violet or Columbia Rose. Reg. 27¢.

F. W. WOOLWORTH CO.

The Millinery Institute Of America Presents Its Spring Collection

An oversized straw picture hat trimmed in giant flowers.

This large sailor is covered with silk roses and stems.

A tall helmet of baby orchids trimmed with grapes and velvet leaves.

This one is made of stiff lace with black velvet ribbon running through it.

An off-the-face turban draped with a long chiffon scarf.

"Easter On Fifth Avenue" is the name of this casino circle of satin ribbon with straw braid.

CRAZY HATS

for Spring from British Columbia

This one is appropriately called a "Double Header."

One of the models from the Chinese YWCA in Vancouver wears "the biggest hat in the world."

HEY LADY... IS THAT A CHICKEN ON YOUR HEAD?

This one is called "Chicken With A Cigarette" and that's no clucking matter.

Shoes

Shoes are fancy with sharply pointed toes and range in fabrics from striped linen, flowered silk crepe and satin to velvet and lace.

Here's What The Experts Say About Wearing High Heels:

TWO HEELS UP

- Physically and psychologically beneficial;

- High Heels throw the weight onto the heel instead of the toe;

- Eliminates slouching;

- Produces more healthy breathing;

- Adds inches to the bust;

- Men love long legs and heels give the impression of greater leg length.

TWO HEELS DOWN

- Produces bow legs and knock knees and the Anti-Cruelty League would protest loudly if men tried to put animals into such a contraption.

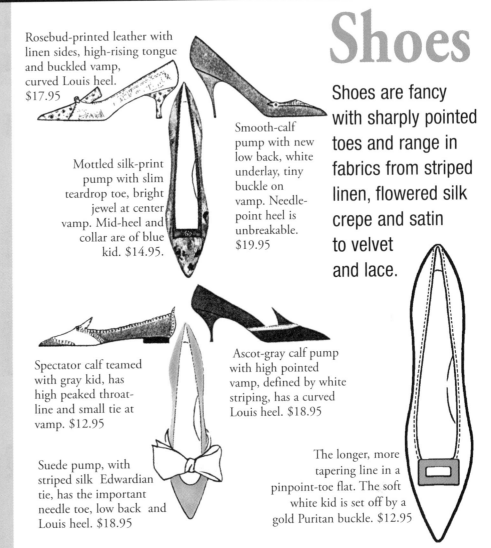

Rosebud-printed leather with linen sides, high-rising tongue and buckled vamp, curved Louis heel. $17.95

Mottled silk-print pump with slim teardrop toe, bright jewel at center vamp. Mid-heel and collar are of blue kid. $14.95.

Smooth-calf pump with new low back, white underlay, tiny buckle on vamp. Needle-point heel is unbreakable. $19.95

Spectator calf teamed with gray kid, has high peaked throat-line and small tie at vamp. $12.95

Suede pump, with striped silk Edwardian tie, has the important needle toe, low back and Louis heel. $18.95

Ascot-gray calf pump with high pointed vamp, defined by white striping, has a curved Louis heel. $18.95

The longer, more tapering line in a pinpoint-toe flat. The soft white kid is set off by a gold Puritan buckle. $12.95

Saddle Shoes are in with the Levis' crowd and casual-wear fans. It doesn't hurt that Elvis Presley makes the scene in a pair of saddle shoes in *Jailhouse Rock*.

The Acapulco High Divers
by Jantzen

Here are three great new Jantzen swimming and diving trunks, improved – and tested – by the famous cliff divers of Acapulco. They fit perfectly, stay comfortable and look good all day,

Jantzen

ur goes to Epsom Downs for
smart, they're "dress-up", too

W BUTTONDOWNS

McGREGOR®

SPORTSWEAR

MENSWEAR

Men are wearing suits made of man-made fibers: lightweight blends of Dacron and fine worsted. Small Glen Plaids seem to be a popular choice, while sports jackets are showing huge plaids and *4 buttons, not 6!* Other fashion moves are Hapi Coats made from Oriental silks and smoking or host jackets. Handkerchiefs are fashionable musts. A bit of fashion-daring is seen in scarves, ties and Ascots in paisley prints. Not to be outdone by the ladies, men take to fake furs!

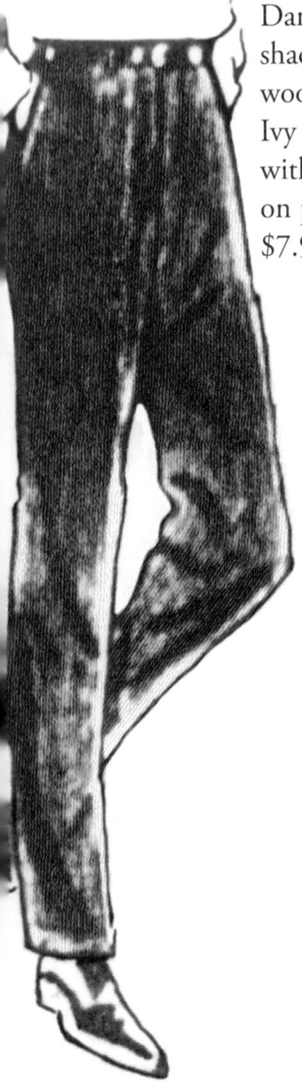

Dark grey shadow-striped wool gabardine Ivy League slacks with leather trim on pockets. $7.95

KANGOL
ONE PIECE

FLEXIBLE CAP

Cotton velvet Host Coat with rayon trim on shawl collar, cuffs and pocket available in dark wine, navy and black. $35.00

Buick SUPER 4-Door Riviera

When better automobiles are built Buick will build them

Roomiest hit in the Style Parade

(Step in and s-t-r-e-t-c-h
—it's the Buick SUPER—and what a dream car to drive!)

WE COULD give you facts and figures, chapter and verse, about the '57 Buick as the *roomiest* of America's best-selling cars.

And that's doubly true of the Buick SUPER pictured here.

Just step into a Buick SUPER—move your arms, relax your shoulders, cross your legs.

Then you'll know comfort that gets sweeter the longer you're there—and styling that looks smarter the longer you stare.

But that's only the start of the thrills you'll find in this most completely changed Buick in history. The real excitement comes from performance that makes this the dream car *to drive.*

Power? You have it, in abundance—for you boss more might than ever gave vigor to a Buick before.

Response? Like nothing in an earth-bound vehicle. For you have the instant action of today's new Dynaflow.*

Ride? Handling? Roadability? Braking? Try 'em and see!

Ask your Buick dealer for a demonstration—and for figures that make Buick your best buy today.

BUICK *Division of* GENERAL MOTORS

New Advanced Variable Pitch Dynaflow is the only Dynaflow Buick builds today. It is standard on Roadmaster, Super and Century—optional at modest extra cost on the Special.

Big Thrill's Buick

SPECIAL · CENTURY · SUPER · ROADMASTER · and ROADMASTER 75

Only Buick brings you this built-in "conscience"
SAFETY-BUZZER

—a simple device that's a great boon to your safety. You merely preset the miles-per-hour you want. When you reach that pace, a warning buzzer sounds. Drop below that pace and the buzzer stops. Standard on ROADMASTER, optional at extra cost on other Series.

Sports

World Series programs

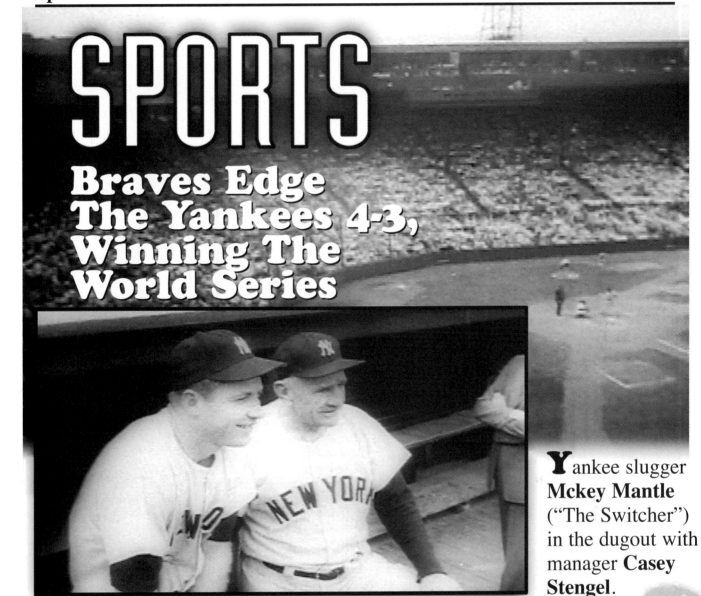

SPORTS

Braves Edge The Yankees 4-3, Winning The World Series

Yankee slugger **Mckey Mantle** ("The Switcher") in the dugout with manager **Casey Stengel**.

Pitcher **Lou Burdette** of the Braves pitches three victories, making Milwaukee the new champions and is named the World Series' Most Valuable Player.

Sam Snead*

You'll Be pleased
when you play
the New

Wilson STAFF !

Cary Middlecoff*

What "STAFF" Means to You

It's called "STAFF" because it is a
development through years of research and
tests by the Wilson staff of playing pro experts...
players like Sam Snead and Cary Middlecoff.

STAFF for '57 is their idea of a dream ball.

This new Wilson STAFF is rifle true in flight.
It looks good...feels good...sounds good...
really goes good.

You're entitled to the best. This year it's
Wilson STAFF. Try it for 18 holes. See why
Middlecoff used it to win the '56 National Open.

SUPERIOR FEATURES of the
new WILSON STAFF BALL

✓ New seamless thin wall center filled with Liquid
X2F for crisper, longer "leap" on each shot.

✓ Special new type vulcanized thread for con-
sistent compression...for greater resilience...
for better impact recovery.

✓ Longer ball...better control.

✓ New markings don't rub or smear.

✓ Sharper, cleaner dimple—never fills in.

✓ A new white paint stays whiter...
and retains gloss longer.

*Member Wilson Advisory Staff

Win With Wilson
. . . .

Wilson Sporting Goods Co., Chicago
Fastest nationwide service from 32 branch offices.
(A subsidiary of Wilson & Co., Inc.)

148

Baseball

SEASON HOME RUN KINGS

HANK AARON
(National League-Milwaukee)
44 Home Runs, 132 Runs Batted In

ROY SIEVERS
(American League-Washington)
42 Home Runs, 114 Runs Batted In

CY YOUNG AWARD

WARREN SPAHN
Milwaukee

MOST VALUABLE PLAYER

AMERICAN LEAGUE
Mickey Mantle
New York Yankees

NATIONAL LEAGUE
Hank Aaron
Milwaukee Braves

NATIONAL LEAGUE BATTING CHAMPION

STAN MUSIAL (St. Louis Cardinals)
.351 Average

AMERICAN LEAGUE BATTING CHAMPION

TED WILLIAMS (Boston Red Sox)
.388 Average

Highest Paid Ball Player
TED WILLIAMS Signs $100,000 Contract With Boston Red Sox.

ROOKIE OF THE YEAR

AMERICAN LEAGUE
Tony Kubek
New York Yankees

NATIONAL LEAGUE
Jack Sanford
Philadelphia Phillies

GO WEST YOUNG MEN-- AND THEY WILL!
New York loses two of its Major League Ball Clubs to the West Coast—the Giants to San Francisco and the Brooklyn Dodgers to Los Angeles.

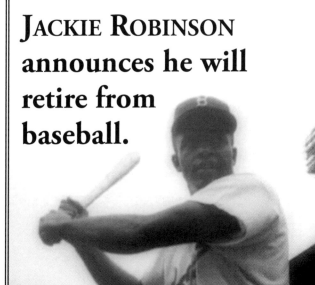

JACKIE ROBINSON announces he will retire from baseball.

149

18,000 Enthusiastic Fans Jam Madison Square Garden To Watch The Contest Between Home Team CCNY And Oregon State.

CCNY scores the first points.

The Northwest team scores again in this close game, much to the chagrin of this CCNY fan.

Some of the players take a spill after Oregon blocks a CCNY attempt at scoring.

The home team boys finally wrap it up, winning 58-51.

Wilt Chamberlain

BASKETBALL

BOSTON CELTICS Beat ST. LOUIS HAWKS 4-3 for the NBA Championship

•

MOST VALUABLE PLAYER OF THE YEAR
Bob Cousy (Boston Celtics)

ROOKIE OF THE YEAR
Tom Heinsohn (Boston Celtics)

NUMBER 1 SCORER
Paul Arizin 1,817 Points

•

NORTH CAROLINA Edges KANSAS 54-53 for the NCAA Championship

•

COLLEGE BOARDS

University of Kansas' **Wilt ("The Stilt") Chamberlain** is the most publicized College Basketball Player in a generation.

With several years of college still ahead of him, Seattle University's **Elgin Baylor** is deluged with professional and industrial-league team offers.

ICE HOCKEY

• **Montreal Canadiens** beat **Boston Bruins** 4-1 for Stanley Cup win.

• **S**weden wins the World and European Championships in Moscow. Protesting Soviet repression of Hungary, the U.S. and Canada are among the nations boycotting the tournament.

Question:

Why does Jack Kramer crave orange juice after a fast tennis match?

Answer:

His Body Wisdom tells him he needs extra Vitamin C and quick energy!

Jack Kramer, world-famed tennis star

Are you active, busy?
Then you need extra orange juice, too!

Stop and count—and you may find you cover as many miles per day as "Mr. Tennis" himself, and use up Vitamin C and energy just as fast. So when *you* have that same craving for a big, cool glass of orange juice, your Body Wisdom is telling you, too, to replenish Vitamin C and energy. You *need*

that extra juice, because—for busy, active people—having it with breakfast is just not enough.

Today, stock up on delicious Fresh-Frozen Orange Juice from Florida. It's rich in Vitamin C; it gives you quick energy. Make an *extra* pitcherful every morning!

This little can makes 4 big glasses!

Less than 5¢ a glass!

© Florida Citrus Commission, Lakeland, Florida, 1957

CHILDREN must have extra juice when they play hard to keep up energy and Vitamin C!

OUTDOOR WORKERS burn up Vitamin C and energy faster, must replace it often!

MOTHERS-TO-BE should double their intake of orange juice for extra Vitamin C!

FRESH-FROZEN ORANGE JUICE *Packed with Florida Sunshine!*

Althea Gibson First African-American To Win Wimbledon & U.S. Nationals

Althea Gibson is congratulated by Darlene Hard after Althea wins the Wimbledon championship.

Althea in action at Forest Hills, NY.

Queen Elizabeth herself presents the symbol of victory to this young woman from Harlem who is now the toast of the tennis world.

Sportsmen everywhere applaud her triumph and share in her moment of victory.

TENNIS

Australia Beats U.S 3-2 To Win Davis Cup.

U.S. OPEN SINGLES CHAMPIONSHIP

Men: **Malcolm Anderson** (over Ashley Cooper)
Women: **Althea Gibson** (over Louise Brough)

WIMBLEDON

Men: **Lew Hoad** (over Ashley Cooper)
Women: **Althea Gibson** (over Darlene Hard)

LOS ANGELES WOMAN WINS AAU DIVING MEET IN HOUSTON

Paula Jean Myers of Los Angeles sweeps all five diving meets.

The beaming winner.

NEW RECORDS IN TRACK & FIELD SET AT THE NCAA MEETS IN AUSTIN, TEXAS

George Bell, of Indiana, sets a new collegiate mark in the broad jump at 26′ 7″.

George changes shoes after his fantastic jump.

ICE SKATING

WORLD FIGURE SKATING CHAMPIONSHIP

Men: David Jenkins (U.S.)

Women: Carol Heiss (U.S.)

U.S. NATIONAL

Men: David Jenkins

Women: Carol Heiss

CANADIAN NATIONAL

Men: Charles Snelling

Women: Carole Jane Pachl

Supreme Court Places Pro Football Under Anti-Trust Laws

Former Syracuse Star, JIM BROWN, Debuts With The Cleveland Browns

FOOTBALL

DETROIT LIONS Beat CLEVELAND BROWNS 59-14 for the NFL Championship

IOWA Trounces OREGON STATE 35-19 Winning the Rose Bowl Competition

NOTRE DAME Beats OKLAHOMA 7-0 Breaking Oklahoma's Four-Year Winning Streak

CANADIAN FOOTBALL LEAGUE CHAMPION (GREY CUP)

Hamilton Tiger-Cats Beat Winnipeg Blue Bombers 32-7

JIM THORPE TROPHY WINNER
Johnny Unitas, Baltimore Colts

John Crow, Texas A&M's All-American halfback is this year's winner of the Heisman Trophy.

"SUGAR" RAY ROBINSON defeats GENE FULLMER, regaining the Middleweight title for the fourth time.

•

CARMEN BASILIO defeats "SUGAR" RAY ROBINSON, winning the Middleweight Boxing Championship.

•

FLOYD PATTERSON beats TOMMY JACKSON in a New York bout, retaining the Heavyweight title.

•

ARCHIE MOORE retains his Light Heavyweight title by knocking out Tony Anthony in the seventh round.

•

Six new members are elected into the Boxing Hall of Fame: CHARLEY MITCHELL, KID MCCOY, PACKY MCFARLAND, LES DARCY, BATTLING NELSON and JOHNNY DUNDEE.

BOXING

AUTO RACING

INDIANAPOLIS 500 WINNER
Sam Hanks (135.601 MPH)

•

WORLD PRIX GRAND CHAMPION
Juan Fangio, Argentina

CYCLING

TOUR DE FRANCE WINNER
Jacques Anquetil (France)

•

UNITED STATES CHAMPION
Jack Disney

•

WORLD CHAMPION
Rik van Steenbergen (Belgium)

RACING

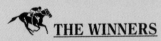 THE WINNERS

KENTUCKY DERBY
"Iron Liege"- Bill Hartack, Jockey
PREAKNESS
"Bold Ruler"- Eddie Arcaro, Jockey
BELMONT STAKES
"Gallant Man"- Willie Shoemaker, Jockey

The First National Wheelchair Games are held at Adelphi College in Garden City, New York including Table Tennis, Javelin and the 60-Yard Dash.

Bill Munsey wins the Speedboat Gold Cup Race on Lake Washington in Seattle.

SWIMMING

Danish Olympic swimming champion **GRETA ANDERSEN** wins the coed race across the English Channel covering the distance in 13 hours and 53 minutes.

U.S. OLYMPIC WINNER BRINGS HOME A BRIDE

After weeks of pleading, American Olympic winner HAROLD CONNOLLY gets approval from the Czech government to allow him to bring his bride, Olympic winner OLGA FIKOTOVA, to the United States. They only have $.35 between them but look forward to a rosy future.

BILLIARDS

World 3-Cushion Champion
Harold Worst, Chicago, Ill.

U.S. Open 3-Cushion Champion
Arthur Rubin, Brooklyn, NY

U.S. Pocket Billiards
Luther Lassiter, Elizabeth City, N.C.

World Pocket Crown
Willie Mosconi, Philadelphia, Pa.

BOWLING

54TH American Bowling Congress Champion
Jim Spalding, Louisville, KY.
Record Score: 2,088

Born in 1957
Evelyn Ashford

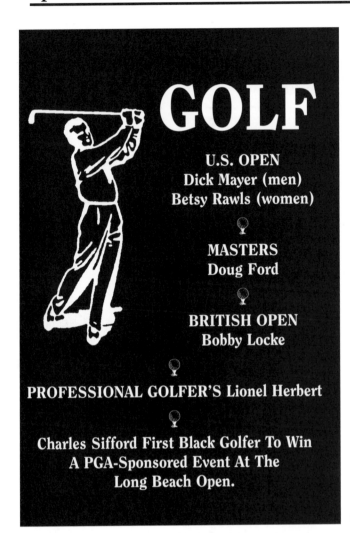

GOLF

U.S. OPEN
Dick Mayer (men)
Betsy Rawls (women)

MASTERS
Doug Ford

BRITISH OPEN
Bobby Locke

PROFESSIONAL GOLFER'S Lionel Herbert

Charles Sifford First Black Golfer To Win A PGA-Sponsored Event At The Long Beach Open.

CHESS

14-Year Old BOBBY FISCHER Becomes Open Champion Of U.S. Chess Federation.

VASSILY SMYSLOV Dethrones MIKHAIL BOTVINNIK'S 9-Year Reign As World Chess Champion.

TRACK & FIELD

London's White City Stadium is the site of the greatest mile race of all time when four runners in the same event run the distance in less than 4 minutes.

University of Pennsylvania track star Bruce Dern resigns from the team rather than shave his sideburns.

The International Olympic Committee Votes to Add Volleyball and Archery to its Sports Line-Up.